**PRINT CASEBOOKS 3/THIRD ANNUAL EDITION
THE BEST IN EXHIBITION DESIGN**

I. S.

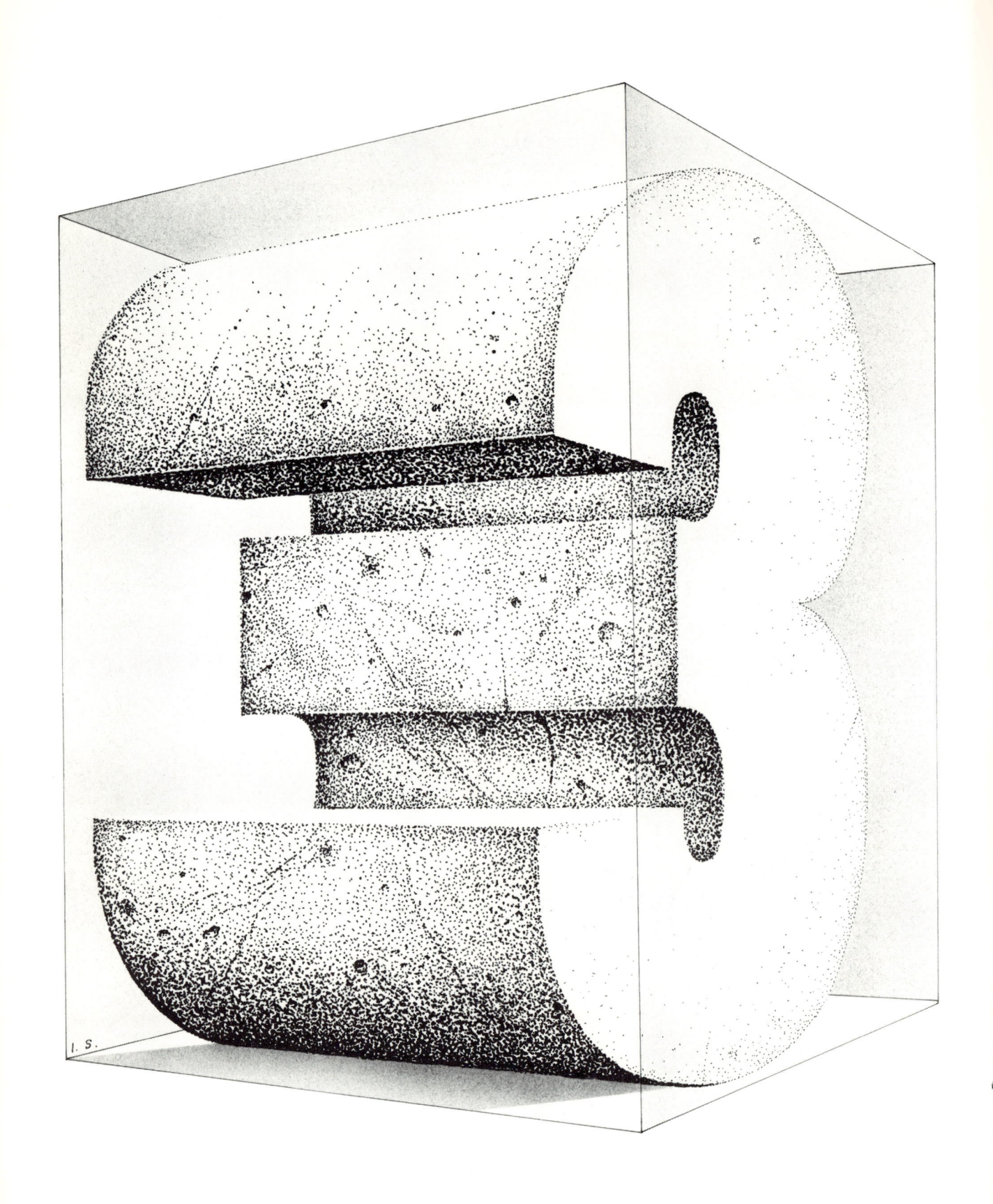

PRINT CASEBOOKS 3
THIRD ANNUAL EDITION
THE BEST IN EXHIBITION DESIGN

Conceived by
Martin Fox

Text and Introduction by
Edward K. Carpenter

Published by
**RC Publications, Inc.
Washington, D.C.**

INTRODUCTION

Copyright © 1978 by RC Publications, Inc. All rights reserved.

Published by RC Publications, Inc.
6400 Goldsboro Road NW
Washington, D.C. 20034

No part of this publication may be reproduced or used in any form or by any means—graphic, electronic, or mechanical, including photocopying, recording, taping, or information storage and retrieval systems—without written permission of the publisher.

Manufactured in U.S.A.
First Printing 1978

PRINT CASEBOOKS 3/THIRD ANNUAL EDITION/THE BEST IN EXHIBITION DESIGN
Library of Congress Catalog Card Number 76-39580
ISBN 0-915734-22-2

PRINT CASEBOOKS 3/THIRD ANNUAL EDITION
Complete 6-Volume Set
ISBN 0-915734-18-4

RC PUBLICATIONS
President and Publisher: Robert Cadel
Vice President and Editor: Martin Fox
Art Director/Designer: Andrew P. Kner
Associate Editor: Teresa Reese
Associate Art Director: Rose M. DeNeve
Business Manager: Howard Cadel
Title Page Illustration: Isadore Seltzer

In the world of exhibitions, if 1976 was the year of the Bicentennial, then 1977 was the year of the museum. Fourteen (of the 24) exhibits shown here appeared in museums. Actually there was some carry-over from '76, for five of these 24 exhibits owed their existence to Bicentennial furor. "Treasures of Tutankhamun," which I am counting as three exhibits since three of its six U.S. installations are included, fits both categories. It came to this country as a Bicentennial gesture from the Egyptian Government, pausing in six museums in its two-and-a-half-year cross-country tour, and catching people's imaginations in a way few exhibits ever have. Certainly no exhibit outside a world's fair or major exposition has drawn such constant crowds, become the subject of so much local chatter, received such intense press coverage, or been the inspiration (catalyst is a better word) for fads in fashion, furniture and fancy.

For exhibit designers the King Tut exhibit posed very real problems in how to handle crowds. At Washington, D.C.'s National Gallery of Art, where the exhibit opened first, crowds were twice what had been expected. By the end of its four-month Washington stay, the exhibit had drawn almost 850,000 visitors. In New Orleans about the same number waited patiently for a chance to see the gold and alabaster Egyptian artifacts; and in Chicago, where the Field Museum allowed 1000 persons into the exhibit at once (vs. 800 at once in both Washington and New Orleans), 1.5 million persons crowded into the exhibit during its four-month stay.

Short of increasing the space allotted per artifact, there is little a designer can do about crowds. Still, setting up an exhibit like the "Treasures of Tutankhamun" in the Astrodome would give it more space but hardly help viewers see it better, nor would mounting everything on a ceiling, clearing floor space, so visitors could stand packed beneath the exhibit, shoulder to shoulder, like stouthearted men, peering up, their sight unobstructed. Limited access to a limited exhibit space is probably the best solution. Ironically, doing that, like limiting entrants to the hottest discotheque, can further spur public enthusiasm.

Why "Treasures of Tutankhamun" so excited the public imagination is a complex question. An exhibit with some of the same artifacts, also titled "Treasures of Tutankhamun," which toured the U.S. for 18 months in 1961 and 1962, playing in twice as many cities, is scarcely remembered now and attracted relatively little notice then. That earlier show had 34 artifacts; 12 reappear in the current rendition. Sponsored by the American Association of Museums, the earlier Tutankhamun exhibit was meant to raise U.S. dander and dollars toward saving archeological treasures from the Aswan Dam that was about to flood 6000 years of Egyptian history.

Probably a large dollop of credit for the current exhibit's excitement goes to Thomas Hoving, former director of New York's Metropolitan Museum of Art. It was his decision to make the exhibit one of discovery, to have it recreate the search for and uncovering of Tutankhamun's tomb by a British archeological team. Certainly Hoving's decision inspired the different designers who mounted the exhibit at each museum.

Two of the three Tutankhamun installations seen in these pages were designed by in-house staffs. Five of all the exhibits included here were done by staff designers, compared to only two last year. This increase perhaps spots a trend: more good work being turned out by institutions and corporations that formerly hired independent design firms. Whether this trend shows a greater awareness of design is questionable. What does seem certain, to judge from the overall level of entries submitted to this Casebook, is that good work is becoming more widespread. In offering a possible explanation for this, exhibit designers I have spoken to agree that, year by year, exhibit-goers appear able to understand and absorb more. This elevating sophistication demands more from the designer, while giving him greater scope. It is perhaps indicative of this greater awareness that a quarter of this year's Casebook exhibits used audio-visual effects—films, slide shows, computer printouts, taped messages, or combinations of all these, and one exhibit, Philadelphia's Living History Center, was set up entirely with audio-visual devices.

George Gardner, a Casebook juror and chairman of exhibitions and graphics at New York's American Museum of Natural History, feels strongly about the use of audio-visual aids in exhibits. "Audio-visual devices are a good way of reaching today's audiences," he says. "Brought up on television, today's young audiences can absorb more from multiple sources than can people who grew up before television. Something that moves, say a snake, a tadpole, a frog, the opening of a chrysalis and the emergence of a butterfly, can be shown on film more effectively than in a diagram or as a mounted artifact." Gardner feels that audio-visual devices can help an audience relate to an exhibit, though, he stresses, they can be overdone.

In general, the jurors felt the Living History Center is overdone. "A multi-million-dollar, multi-media orgasm," one of them called it. And while they praised its spatial arrangement and the way crowds were allowed to take in other parts of the exhibit while waiting for the main film, they felt that too much goes on in the single building. Their reluctance to endorse it without qualification stemmed from its overloading of the senses, not its violation of tradition by failing to include artifacts and more than minimal text.

More traditional critics *did* object to the lack of artifacts. A voice reading the Bill of Rights or the Declaration of Independence cannot substitute for the presentation

5/Exhibition Design

of the original document, they argued. Similarly, a film of Jasper Johns painting cannot replace the actual presence of one of his completed works. But perhaps mass recreations of events and objects have blurred our perception until the TV image has become the only real one. War on television is more real to us than the one actually going on 10,000 miles away. If this is true, then the only artifact worth having is the one of the TV screen. It may be this realization that the traditionalists are fighting.

Speaking in a slightly different context, Etan Manasse, who is chairman of Pratt Institute's Visual Communication Department, once noted that museum exhibits are becoming events, produced quickly after a discovery. He was talking specifically of a paper model of a giant flying reptile that appeared in the American Museum of Natural History only weeks after the real skeleton was unearthed. The next step, Manasse projected, "will be an exhibit that's an actual video transmission of the excavation." It makes one shudder slightly to realize that, if Howard Carter had unearthed Tutankhamun's tomb in 1972 instead of 1922, he might well have had a TV crew behind him as he first peered into the burial chamber.

In any case, TV, slides, and films have far from taken over this batch of Casebook exhibits. The most striking is "Treasures of Tutankhamun," an exhibit presented solely by a combination of artifacts and designers' art.

Only two innovations showed up this year as jurors spent most of a day viewing over 1000 slides. One was the computer which The Burdick Group designed into a nutrition exhibit at Chicago's Museum of Science and Industry. Visitors can feed the computer personal statistics and ask it about their own nutrition. With the computer the exhibit holds an average visitor for 20 minutes. Bruce Burdick's use of the computer was perhaps foreshadowed by Carlos Ramirez and Albert H. Woods, Inc.'s traveling exhibit for IBM, "Talk With a Computer," shown in the previous Exhibition Design Casebook. Like a caged vaudeville performer, the computer, which answered visitor's questions, *was* the exhibit.

The other innovation is the creation of open museum storage. The University of British Columbia's recently completed Museum of Anthropology puts its study collection in glass cases and drawers, right off the main exhibit galleries, making it accessible to a layman, professional scholar, or anyone else. In the redesign of its Egyptian galleries, the Metropolitan Museum of Art is doing the same thing, putting all the artifacts in its Egyptian collection on display.

Innovation is being rediscovered in the use of typefaces. Though it is too early to call it a trend, exhibit designers seem to be turning from a blanket use of Helvetica. Fourteen of the 24 exhibits here (or roughly three out of five) use a typeface other than Helvetica, and designers show signs of experimenting, of turning to a range of other typefaces. Two use Century Schoolbook, two use Souvenir, the rest feature a scattering of individual faces. Asked why he had chosen a particular typeface, one designer said, among other things, "to get away from Helvetica."

Again, this year, money has little to do with good design. The budgets for exhibits seen here range from the $1.8 million spent by Raymond Loewy International on the Living History Center's exhibit to the $600 spent by two Washington University graduate students on an exhibit of student work.

Five of these exhibits are Bicentennial exhibits, but the rest show the usual range of exhibit work. Only one is a trade show exhibit, produced by the Corning Glass design department for Corning Housewares. Five are corporate exhibits, two are student exhibits, three are government shows, and, as I've noted, 14 are in museums.

Most of the current exhibit devices appear. Corning Housewares even had James Beard at work, cooking, in its exhibit space at Chicago's McCormick Place. But Casebook juror Barry Howard, for one, missed seeing more experimentation. "No one," he mused, "is putting people in an environment where they are enveloped by the exhibit."

—*Edward K. Carpenter*

CASEBOOK JURORS

Dick Lopez

Dick Lopez, president and founder of the graphic design firm of Lopez Salpeter, Inc., New York City, graduated from the School of Industrial Art in 1959, later studied architecture at Pratt Institute and the City University of New York. He started as an apprentice designer for Walter Dorwin Teague Associates and, after a series of jobs with other firms and a stint as a freelancer, he established his own firm, Dimensional Concepts, Inc., in 1969, retaining business acquaintance Bob Salpeter as creative consultant. When Salpeter joined the partnership, the company was renamed and has since expanded to include corporate identity programs, annual reports, booklets and brochures, films, advertising, packaging, slide presentations and exhibitions.

Exhibition Design/6

David Strong

After majoring in commercial art and industrial design at the University of Washington, Strong freelanced in Seattle and in 1962 became the art director for Douglas Fir Plywood Association; he executed the identity program when the group changed its name to the American Plywood Association. Four years later, Strong was retained by the Weyerhaeuser Company to help organize a major identification change and was responsible for development of an identity guidelines manual and the design of formats for all company material from signs and letterheads to product labels. He established his own Seattle-based firm, David Strong Design Group, in 1968.

Albert H. Woods

After receiving his BA in Industrial Design from Auburn University, Woods was employed by several firms, first in Chicago, then New York. He worked with Charles Eames on the introductory multiple-image film for the U.S. Science Pavilion at the Seattle World's Fair and with Francis Thompson on a multiple-image film on the work of R. Buckminster Fuller. In 1966 he went into partnership and formed Carlos Ramirez & Albert H. Woods, Inc. The firm's initial project was the Canadian Government's Expo '67 Theme Pavilion, "Man and his Resources," an exhibit embodying films, interactive exhibits and interior architecture. Later came commissions from major corporations and city, state and federal governments, both national and international.

Barry Howard

Barry Howard has been engaged in exhibition, exposition and interpretive design projects for more than 20 years. He is the principal of Barry Howard & Associates, Inc., Scarsdale, NY, and among the projects he has been actively involved with are the American Freedom Train, the California State Railroad Museum, the National Environmental Visitor Center, and a wide range of museum and interpretive facilities for the U.S. National Park Service, the U.S. Army Corps of Engineers, and many other federal and state agencies.

George S. Gardner

As chairman of the exhibition and graphics department of the American Museum of Natural History, Gardner is responsible for design and construction of permanent halls and temporary exhibits on dinosaurs, minerals, butterflies, and the like. The annual budget for this exhibition program is more than $1.1 million. He is currently developing an overall graphic redesign program for all directional and information signing at the American Museum. Gardner was curator of exhibits at the Hall of Fame of the Trotter in Goshen, NY, from 1970-73. He was a partner in the design firm of Yang/Gardner for 12 years and before that worked with Walter Dorwin Teague.

7/Exhibition Design

CASEBOOK WRITER

Edward K. Carpenter

A writer on various aspects of architecture and design, Carpenter has been an editor for Industrial Design and Progressive Architecture, a correspondent-at-large for the Architectural Forum, and is currently a contributing editor of Urban Design and PRINT magazines. He wrote *Casebooks 2/Best in Exhibition Design* and *Casebooks 1/Best in Environmental Graphics*. Carpenter's most recent book is *Urban Design Case Studies*.

INDEX Exhibitions

Celebrate '76 **61**
Corning Housewares **21**
Design Education at Pratt Institute **24**
Egyptian Reinstallation Phase I **92**
Fire! **48**
Food for Life **66**
Graphic Communications Student Show **38**
Greek Pavilion **44**
History of Rocketry and Space Flight **35**
IBM's Architecture and Artifacts **79**
IBM's Flexible Exhibition System **73**
IBM's Permanent Exhibition on the History of Computing **76**
Living History Center **27**
MAN transFORMS **31**
Maps: Their Art and Their Science **70**
Montreal Museum of Fine Arts **56**
Museum of Anthropology, University of British Columbia **82**
Natural Science **87**
Saga of the Great Plains **41**
Satellites Hall **52**
Theatrical Set for Sports Illustrated **90**
Treasures of Tutankhamun **10**

Exhibition Design/8

Clients/Sponsoring Organizations

Design Firms/Designers/Consultants

Academy of Natural Science **87**
American Museum of Natural History **70**
British Columbia, University of **82**
Cooper-Hewitt Museum **31**
Corning Glassworks **21**
Esmark/Swift & Co. **66**
Field Museum of Natural History **15**
Greek Government **44**
IBM Corp. **73, 76**
IBM General Services Div. **79**
International Communication Agency **41**
Montreal Museum of Fine Arts **56**
Morton, Jack, Productions **90**
National Air and Space Museum, Smithsonian Institution **35, 52**
National Gallery of Art **10**
New Orleans Museum of Art **18**
Philadelphia '76, Inc. **27**
Pratt Institute **24**
Rockefeller Center, Inc. **61**
Washington University, Graphic Communications Dept. **38**
Western Forestry Center **48**

Adams, Franklin **18**
Altieri, John, & Associates **92**
Anderson, Roy **41**
Appelbaum, Ralph **27**
Arcop Architects **56**
Ardalan, Nader **31**
Balisky, Vince **48**
Barna, Peter **52**
Bell, Randall **35**
Bergen Expo Systems **27**
Binette & Associates **44**
Bode, Peter M. **31**
Bogue Babicki and Associates **82**
Borella, David **38**
British Columbia, University of, Dept. of Anthropology **82**
Brunell, Richard **38**
Burdick, Bruce **66**
Burdick Group, The **66**
Cooper, Margaret **70**
Corning Design **21**
Courchesnes, Luc **44, 56**
de Capra, DeLuca **76**
de Harak, Rudolph **92**
Demers, Guy **44**
Dimitri, Dimakopoulos & Associates **44**
Donovan, Michael **70**
Donovan & Green, Inc. **70**
Erickson, Arthur, Architects **82**
Fellowes, Lucy **31**
Field Museum of Natural History, Dept. of Exhibition **15**
Fiorentino, Imero, Associates **27**
Fisher, Jim **48**
Freedman, David **24**
Freid, Ethel **41**
Fuller, R. Buckminster **31**
Gauthier, Denis **56**
Gelberg, Murry **27**
Globus, Dorothy Twining **31**
Green, Nancy **70**
Grigor, Murray **31**
Guillon, Jacques S. **44**
Guillon, Jacques/Designers, Inc. **44, 56**
Haggert, W.T., & Co. Ltd. **82**
Hamilton, Stephen **66**
Harenstein, Sidney **70**
Hechinger, Nancy **27**

Herbst/LaZar Design, Inc. **35**
Hicks, Linda **41**
Hoefel, Gene **38**
Hollein, Hans **31**
Hopping, Kovach & Grinnel Associates **82**
Hunter, Edward **41**
ICA Exhibit Design Staff **41**
Isozaki, Arata **31**
Janus, Tom **90**
Johnston, Judy **52**
Klein, Larry **15**
Kissiloff, William **61**
Kissiloff Associates, Inc. **61**
Kovach, Rudy **82**
Kozak, Ben **15**
Kramer, Andrew **66**
Labastrou, Roger **56**
LaComa, Gary **48**
Latham, Stolow **56**
LaZar, Ralph **35**
Lee, Steven **24**
Lerner, David **31**
Levine, Elisabeth **24**
Loewy, Raymond, International **27**
Lott, Dick **82**
Lynch Industries **27**
Manasse, Etan **24**
Manasse, Etan, Associates, Inc. **24**
Manwaring, Michael **21**
Maricich, Joe **48**
Marquart, Laurent **44, 56**
McCarthy, Thomas **48**
McLennan, Bill **82**
Meier, Richard **31**
Millet, Gerald **21**
Natale, Arthur **70**
National Gallery Dept. of Design & Installation **10**
Nelson, George **31**
Oberlander, Cornelia Hahn **82**
Olvera, James **38**
Ramirez, Carlos **73, 76, 79, 87, 90**
Ramirez, Carlos, & Albert H. Woods, Inc. **73, 76, 79, 87, 90**
Ravenel, Gaillard F. **10, 18**
Reis, Gerald **21**
Reithlingshoefer, Don **52**

Robinson, Gordon **82**
Roche, Kevin **92**
Roche, Kevin, John Dinkeloo & Associates **92**
Schiller, Carl **52**
Schlamminger, Karl **31**
Schmid, John **52**
Schmid, John, Associates **52**
Severud Associates **92**
Sexton, George **10, 18**
Shank, Sandra **41**
Shepard, Liz **15**
Simon, Bill **52**
Skeene, Tim **56**
Smith, Morley L. **44, 56**
Smith, Ted **38**
Smyth, Frances P. **10**
Sottsass, Ettore **31**
Spectrum Studios **48**
Strong, David **48**
Strong, David, Design Group **48**
Tardif, Pierre **56**
Tinen, Jay **35**
Toti, Michael J. **38**
Ungers, Oswald Mattias **31**
Vorhes, John **41**
Whitney, Mike **38**
Woodburn, Mellissa **35**
Woods, Albert H. **87**

9/Exhibition Design

Treasures of Tutankhamun

What is perhaps the most dramatic exhibit of ancient art ever seen in the U.S., and certainly one of the most beautiful, began moving across the country in the fall of 1976 and would continue until the spring of 1979. Before returning to Egypt's Cairo Museum where it originated, "The Treasures of Tutankhamun" was scheduled to appear in six major U. S. museums and be viewed by an estimated 6.5 million persons. On display were 55 objects from King Tutankhamun's tomb, sent here by Egypt as a Bicentennial gesture. Not incidentally, under the U.S. agreement with Egypt, net proceeds from the sale of printed material and reproductions at each U.S. museum goes to the Organization of Egyptian Antiquities for major renovation work at the Cairo Museum and for similar, but less extensive, work at Alexandria's Greco-Roman Museum.

At a January 1976 meeting in Chicago's Field Museum of Natural History, designers and curators from the six U.S. museums hosting the show learned what objects would be sent, that they would be accompanied by photomurals of the discovery of King Tut's tomb and its contents and by panels of explanatory text, and that the Egyptian government wanted the objects displayed in four basic groups, in the order of their discovery in the tomb's four areas: antechamber, burial chamber, treasury and annex. Gaillard F. Ravenel of the National Gallery of Art would select photos for the photomurals, and ferret out accompanying quotations from archeologist Howard Carter's three-volume journal of his search for and discovery of Tutankhamun's tomb. The designers agreed that each museum would do its own labeling and that each would display the artifacts in plexiglass cases on pedestals.

Gaillard Ravenel, Stuart Silver of New York's Metropolitan Museum, and David Silverman of the Oriental Institute organized the exhibit. But it was Thomas Hoving, then director of the Metropolitan Museum of Art, the show's U.S. sponsor, who made the most inspired decision: to make the exhibit one of discovery, to explain Carter's quest for the tomb and its gold and alabaster treasure. Carter's discovery, financed by the Earl of Carnarvon, was probably the most spectacular archeological event of the 20th century. And it is the drama of the recreated event as much as the beauty of the objects that caught the public's fancy during 1977.

As if inspired by this drama, the exhibit designers took Hoving's concept and Tutankhamun's burial accouterments and intensified the appeal of both. The singular beauty of the 55 artifacts makes this a textbook example of a Beautiful Artifact Exhibit. Their beauty could have become a restraint. The designer's role could have become what Ed Sullivan's was on television... a pointer, critics called him, someone who points to someone else's talent. It would have been easy and not without logic to let the objects speak for themselves. That, however, did not happen in the three installations seen here. (By the time this book went to press, "Treasures of Tutankhamun" had played in only three of its six scheduled stops—Washington, Chicago and New Orleans. It subsequently moved on to Los Angeles, Seattle and—its final stop—New York. Though it was obvious no setting could intrude on the artifacts' beauty, there were no other restraints on what the designers could do with background, space, lighting, and positioning of cases, text and photomurals. Each designer manipulated these elements to create an ambience that heightened the exhibit's emotional effect.

National Gallery of Art, Washington, D.C.

The National Gallery opened the initial installation of "Treasures of Tutankhamun" without knowing what to expect in the way of public response. Even had Gaillard F. Ravenel and his designers in the National Gallery's department of design and installation known that the exhibit would draw 835,924 visitors in its four-month Washington stay, there was not really much they could have done about it. As it was, the designers created 12,000-sq. ft. of space in a series of 11 galleries of marvelously varied shapes, strung together like pearls in a necklace by low-doorwayed, narrow, brief, connecting passages. These passages, while heightening the exhibit's drama, may have caused a slowdown of movement through the galleries. However, in none of the three installations described here did crowds move quickly through the exhibit. The average time spent by a visitor to the National Gallery's Tut installation was a little over an hour—about the same as time spent in New Orleans, slightly less than Chicago—and indeed that much time was needed to take it in. Almost everyone read the text panels carefully, and it is a credit to those who organized the exhibit (especially Ravenel and Hoving) that it held visitors enthralled long after they left the museum.

Ravenel selected photos for the murals and supervised their enlargement. It was, of course, fortunate that the Metropolitan Museum had

Exhibition Design/10

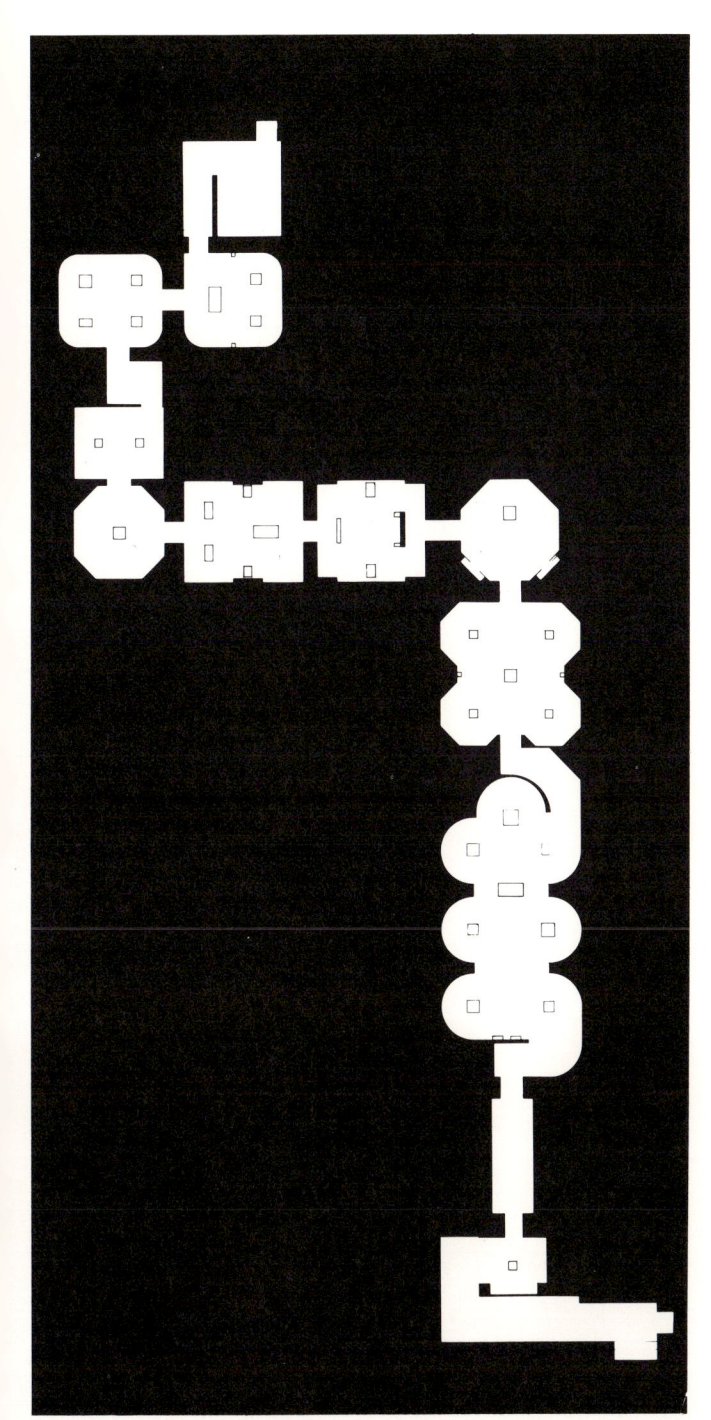

1. National Gallery of Art exhibit space was series of multiform chambers strung together by low, narrow passages.
2. Entrance to National Gallery installation.

11/Exhibition Design

loaned photographer Harry Burton to Lord Carnarvon for the 1922 expedition and had the photographs in storage. But Ravenel's selection of Burton's photos (and of newspaper photos of the event) is brilliant, as is his editing of quotations from Carter's journal. As a result, visitors at the National Gallery —and elsewhere during the U.S. tour—saw what Carter saw as he entered the tomb and read statements of his feelings.

Reading these quotations nudged visitors' curiosity and led them to read panels of explanatory text (also prepared for travel by the National Gallery) positioned throughout the exhibit.

Ravenel and his staff placed emphasis, in each gallery, on the artifacts, giving these objects the best positions and the brightest lighting. Photomurals and explanatory panels were presented as secondary and almost always kept out of a viewer's line of sight as he approached an encased object. The lure that drew visitors from one space to the next in the National Gallery was the view, through a low doorway, of yet another gold or alabaster object in the room beyond.

The designers placed photomurals and explanatory panels on walls at either side of the artifacts. With her outstretched arms the statue of a tutelary goddess seemed, for instance, to welcome an approaching visitor. Once in front of her, visitors saw a photomural at one side showing her standing before the Canopic shrine—as she

3. Photos of tomb's antechamber curve around cases holding antechamber artifacts.
4. Photo of tomb's treasury mounted on case containing treasury artifacts.
5. Wall-mounted text panel explains statuettes, found in treasury.
6. Tutankhamun's golden death mask.

4.

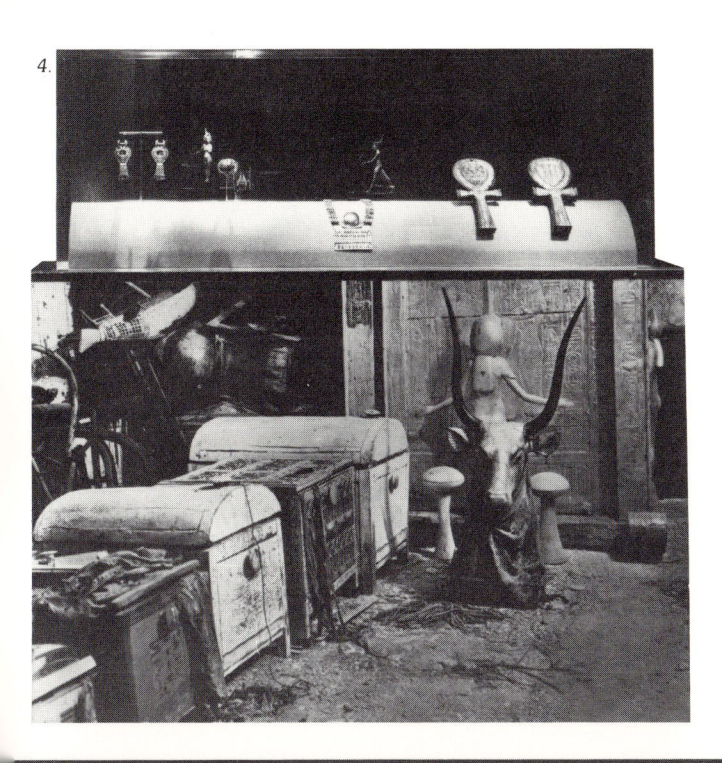

5.

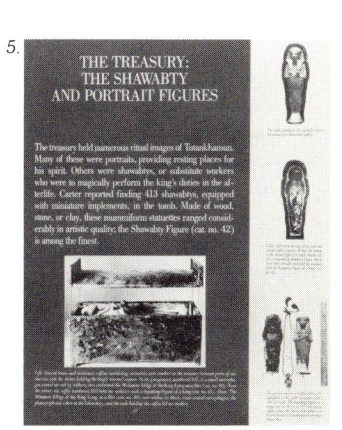

THE TREASURY: THE SHAWABTY AND PORTRAIT FIGURES

The treasury held numerous ritual images of Tutankhamun. Many of these were portraits, providing resting places for his spirit. Others were shawabtys, or substitute workers who were to magically perform the king's duties in the afterlife. Carter reported finding 413 shawabtys, equipped with miniature implements, in the tomb. Made of wood, stone, or clay, these mummiform statuettes ranged considerably in artistic quality; the Shawabty Figure (cat. no. 42) is among the finest.

6.

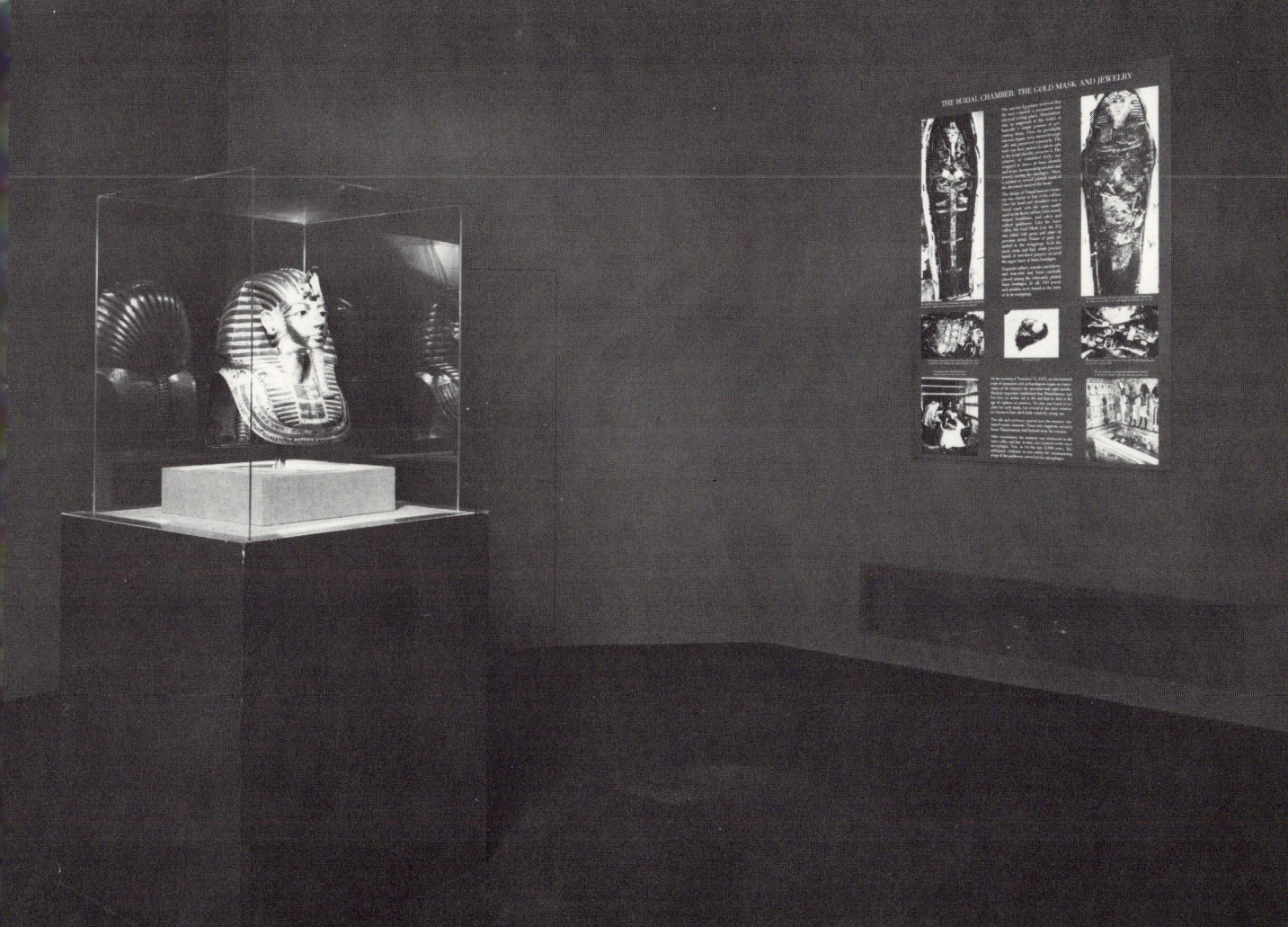

was when Carter found her.

"...a large shrine-shaped chest, completely overlaid with gold, and surmounted by a cornice of sacred cobras. Surrounding this, freestanding, were statues of the four tutelary goddesses of the dead... one felt it almost sacrilege to look at them," reads the excerpt from Howard Carter's journal, set in Bodoni type above the 10'-high photomural.

In one striking instance Ravenel positioned a photomural on a case's base, directly beneath some artifacts. But even here the light was strongest on the artifacts, pieces of jewelry, found in the treasure-laden chests, seen in the photomural in front of the Canopic shrine.

Within the exhibit the 11 galleries are hexagonal, rectangular, and a variety of shapes that defy terminology, some with rounded walls, some with combinations of rounded and straight walls, as if cylinders had been fused with cubes. Only a few artifacts were shown in any one gallery. Throughout, dark colors, lowered doorways, darkened rooms with cases standing in pools of light gave a sense of being somewhere special, a tomb perhaps, or perhaps, as one designer put it, "of not being anywhere but a dark, enclosed space" suspended in time.

Cases designed by Ravenel and his staff have plexiglass vitrines on bases of linen-covered plywood. These bases were filled with cinder blocks for stability and then bolted to metal plates in the floor.

Client: National Gallery of Art
Design firm: National Gallery Department of Design and Installation
Designers: Gaillard F. Ravenel, George Sexton, Frances P. Smyth
Writer: William J. Smith
Fabricators: Corning Construction; Design & Production, Inc.; Russell William Ltd.; Metropolitan Museum of Art and National Gallery conservation staffs; General Type, Inc.

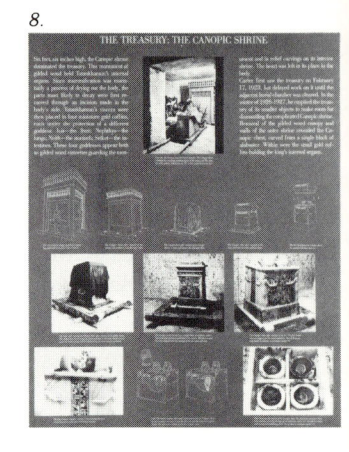

7, 8. Wall panels.
9. Antechamber photomurals define passage between galleries.

Field Museum of Natural History, Chicago

A visitor had to wait some four and a half hours (about two hours in line outside the museum, then approximately two and a half more, out of line, inside) before being admitted to the Field Museum of Natural History's exhibit of "Treasures of Tutankhamun." According to a Field Museum survey, almost half these visitors (40.7 per cent) started lining up outside each morning before seven a.m. The Field made the wait somewhat palatable by letting visitors exchange their museum entrance receipts, once inside, for King Tut Exhibition passes. Each pass carried a number and visitors could wander through the museum, shopping, visiting other exhibits and collections, pausing for coffee, until their number appeared on TV monitors scattered throughout the museum. Using electronic monitors at the exhibit's entrance and exit, museum personnel kept the number of persons inside the exhibit constant. "Our goal was 1000 visitors per hour," writes Larry Klein, chairman of the Field Museum's department of exhibition. "At times crowds inside numbered 1150. This was too many." (Visitors averaged one hour 42 minutes in the exhibit.)

Though nobody liked the crowds, the crowds kept coming, until by the end of the exhibit's four-month stay, 1½ million—a number equalling almost half Chicago's population—had trooped across the exhibit's warm-brown-gray wool carpet. "There's not really much a designer can do about crowds," says Ben Kozak, the Field's senior designer on the Tut installation. "We positioned the cases about 6' to 8' apart, so people could be standing at either of two cases and other people could still pass between them." The designers also left plenty of space (approximately 650 sq. ft. out of a total exhibit space of roughly 13,000 sq. ft.) for the two plexiglass cases holding the exhibit's star attractions... the King's golden death mask and the golden necklace known as the vulture pectoral. The death mask stood higher than any other artifact. This height—chin-high on an average viewer—assured everyone a good view. It also honored the mandate that a king's eyes be above yours so he can see into your thoughts.

Further, Kozak designed each base, on which objects sat within the sealed plexiglass vitrines, with all four sides angled inward and upward at 45-degree angles. On these sloping surfaces the designers positioned labeling text, so an object could be identified at a distance by viewers on all sides of the cases. In some areas Klein and Kozak clustered cases so that viewers could drift off to a nearby case if the crowd around any one became too inhibiting.

In line with his strong feeling that a designer must be involved in all phases of his design ("You can't divorce graphics from spatial arrangement or either one from lighting," he says), Kozak did his own lighting for the Tut installation. He placed spotlights on the perimeter of

1, 2. Field Museum announces Tut exhibit with banners and posters.

1.

2.

15/Exhibition Design

acoustical tile canopies, dropped 10′ above the floor, beneath 20′ ceilings, over individual cases. These canopies were either 4′ by 4′ or 4′ by 8′ depending on the sizes of the cases beneath. Since the lighting was relatively close to the floor, the entire ceiling disappeared behind it, and the effect became that of a low-ceilinged room. Painted a dark blue-gray, similar panels covered the walls. Their rough texture seemed almost like rock, the rock of an Egyptian tomb. To blend the cases into the exhibit area, Kozak ran the wool carpeting up the sides of the pedestal bases.

With some care Kozak positioned low-voltage, high-intensity lights to spot each object. The lighting had to be delicate, he explains, because "if gold is illuminated too strongly it looks like brass; if alabaster and ivory are lit too strongly they look like plastic." Still, he had to keep the light-level high enough so that people could read blocks of text and not stumble into one another. Kozak spent a good deal of time hand-grinding his spotlights' individual plexiglass filters. When he had finished, areas within each filter focused intense beams on features of the objects below that he wanted highlighted, while light passing through the rest of the filter softly washed the object and the case.

Lighting lent considerable drama to the exhibit entrance. Visitors entered from a 1590-sq. ft. orientation area where text and photomurals told of the work that preceded the tomb's discovery. Here, the lighting was bright, intense, desert-like. Straight incandescent spots lit the graphic panels. On the walls a high-level spot shone through a yellow filter, washing the gray walls. To intensify the feeling of being in the desert, the designers painted a false horizon, a ridge line, on the walls. This horizon continued as one moved from the orientation area into a long passageway leading to the exhibit's four chambers. As one made a right-angle turn in front of the photomural of the unearthed tomb entrance and started down the 156′-long, 8′-wide entrance corridor, the horizon line was at floor level. Gradually it rose to 3′6″ at the first exhibit chamber's entrance. Acoustical panel canopies, eight in all, each holding lights that illuminated the floor, rose in height from 6′6″ as one entered the passage to 10′ above the floor as one entered the first chamber, the antechamber. It was like actually entering a tomb.

Having passed through the exhibit spaces with their dim ambient lighting, one moved past photos of the tomb's contents being hauled to Cairo and into a brightly lighted, bazaar-like sales area.

Larry Klein and his staff had a budget of $327,000, which didn't include their salaries, and 15 months in which to complete the installation.

Client: Field Museum of Natural History
Design firm: Department of Exhibition, Field Museum of Natural History
Designers: Larry Klein, Ben Kozak, Liz Shepard
Fabricators: Russell William Ltd. (vitrines); General Exhibits & Displays, Inc.

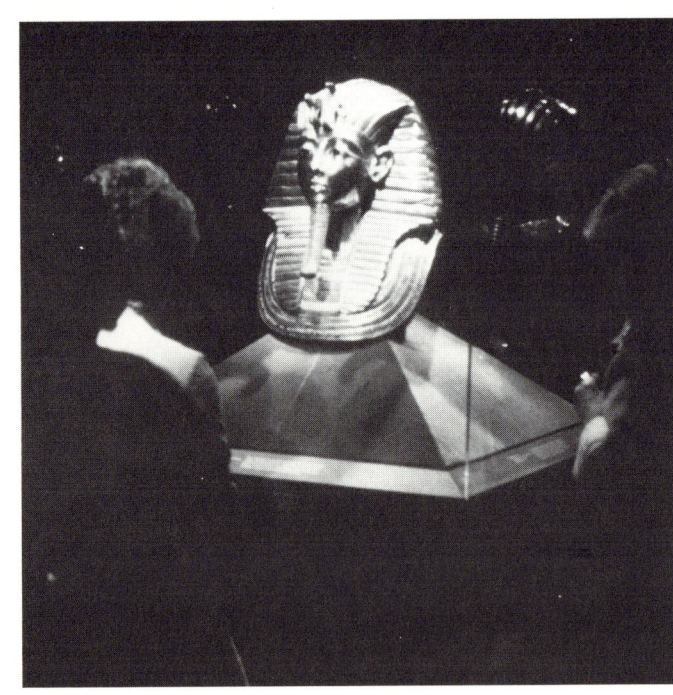

Entrance to Field Museum Tut
installation with photomural of tomb
entrance beyond electronic counters.
Golden death mask.
Gray carpeting covers sides of artifact
cases.
Hand-ground lenses in ceiling spots
highlight specific portions of artifacts.

5.

6.

New Orleans Museum of Art

"Vistas are important to me," says Franklin Adams, who designed the New Orleans Museum of Art's installation for "Treasures of Tutankhamun." "I put more thought and effort into vistas than into other items." To display the 55 artifacts from King Tut's tomb, Adams fashioned halls and chambers from 22,000 sq. ft. of gypsum board, painted dark gray. Visitors moved between the six chambers, where these artifacts were displayed (in 46 plexiglass cases borrowed from the National Gallery), through low-browed portals and a chain of connecting passages. For the most part, Adams separated artifacts and photomurals, placing the photomurals in the connecting passageways, where they served as a transition and a lure. These murals showed Tutankhamun's treasure-laden tomb as it appeared when excavated by a British archaeological team led by Howard Carter. Quotations from Carter's journals told the story of his search for and discovery of the tomb.

"I wanted Carter's statements to be easy to read, as close to eye-level as possible," says Adams. Sometimes these texts were silk-screened directly to walls adjacent to accompanying 10'-high photomurals. More frequently Adams screened them above low portals. Through the portal one saw the photomural showing what Carter was reacting to. As visitors moved through the portal, the mural would block their way, and they would turn to face another open vista. At the end of this new axis would be a case holding an artifact from the scene in the photomural.

"At first I could see nothing ... but presently, as my eyes grew accustomed to the light ... details of the room within emerged slowly from the mist, strange animals, statues, and gold—everywhere the glint of gold," wrote Carter. Adams positioned this block of text (set in Melior typeface) above a low portal between the entrance passageway and an antechamber. Beyond the portal was a three-panel photomural (10' high and 24' long) of the burial chamber Carter was describing.

In this way visitors were constantly pulled through the exhibit, moving from text to photomural to artifacts, and on to the next alluring bit of text and glimpse of photomural.

Lighting helped the drama. Plexiglass cases were spotlighted in otherwise darkened areas, surrounded by dark gray walls and carpets. If not tomb-like, the atmosphere was hushed and dramatic. Even before glimpsing the artifacts, visitors could tell they were witnessing something romantic and mysterious.

Adams had the advantages of Gil Ravenel's advice and of seeing the National Gallery installation before the exhibit arrived in New Orleans, and he knew that the show's greatest crowd-pleasers were Tutankhamun's gold burial mask and jewelry. Adams let these items stand alone, with nothing else around them. Elsewhere he decided to space cases, which he often

1.

1. Entrance to the New Orleans Tut installation.
2. Photomurals lure visitors through the exhibit.
3. Plexiglass cases are 7' apart.

> Six full seasons we had excavated there, and season after season had drawn a blank. We had almost made up our minds that we were beaten, and were preparing to leave The Valley...and then... hardly had I arrived on the work next morning than the unusual silence, due to the stoppage of the work, made me realize that something out of the ordinary had happened, and I was greeted by the announcement that a step cut in the rock had been discovered.
>
> HOWARD CARTER,
> NOVEMBER 4, 1922

presented in clusters, no closer than 7' apart, the amount of space, he felt, that would be taken by viewers at each of two cases and someone moving between them. "I wanted to make people comfortable," he explains.

Once the exhibit opened, Adams learned that New York's Metropolitan Museum gives crowds in high-traffic shows only one thing to look at at a time, in an effort to keep people moving, and leaves more space at the beginning of an exhibit, where people tend to spend more time, and less room at the end. "We're not used to crowds," explains Adams. "The only other time the New Orleans Museum had traffic this heavy was for the moon rocks."

Given the relaxed, polite New Orleans crowds, Adams' traffic flow worked adquately. Would he change anything if he had it to do again? He frets about auxilliary equipment such as emergency lighting and hydrothermographs that had to be in each exhibit space and which he feels now he should have concealed. "I thought about the fire extinguishers and put them in niches," he says; "but though I put the emergency lights and hydrothermographs up near the ceiling, they were out in the open. I would have put a wall or a scrim in front of them." No one noticed, of course; few visitors walk through *any* exhibit looking at the ceiling. But Adams feels any foreign elements in an exhibit space "register subliminally," conditioning viewers' attitudes toward an exhibit.

4, 5. Tutankhamun's death mask stands separately, dramatically framed by portal between exhibit galleries.

Client: New Orleans Museum of Art
Designer: Franklin Adams, New Orleans
Consultants: Gaillard F. Ravenel, George Sexton
Fabricator: Carl E. Woodward Co.

Exhibition Design/20

Corning Housewares

Twice each year in Chicago's vast McCormick Place, Corning Glassworks displays its products to its dealers and competitors. Corning usually has a new item to add to its glassware and kitchenware lines or a new suggestion for its dealers about product display. But the exhibits do more than just display kitchenware in bright, fresh settings.

In the recent installation, shown here, Corning built a kitchen in part of its 1500-sq. ft. space, and had James Beard and others from New York's Good Cooks Cooking School give hourly demonstrations of cooking with Corning cooking utensils and appliances.

Next to the kitchen, Corning designer Gerald Millet positioned a 10' by 15' open platform from which visitors could watch Beard cook (and help sample his results). Between cooking shows, salesmen used the area to chat with visitors and hand out Corning literature.

Beard, his fellow cooks and their cooking odors were an obvious lure. When they weren't present the Corning display relied on what the Casebook jurors called the "elegance, taste and restraint" of its exhibit devices and on its "beautiful graphics."

To create the display, Millet suspended a steel grid (Unistrut) 12' off the floor; from this grid he hung blind-bolted, hollow birch boxes, which stretched almost to the floor. Painted white and silk-screened with supergraphics of various foods, these 12' by 6' by 2' boxes became lures, and in some cases, display devices.

1, 2. Corning Glassworks products and packages line shelves on wooden panels positioned between floor and a Unistrut grid system. Supergraphics of food become a backdrop.

21/Exhibition Design

On their outer, lower surfaces Millet occasionally hung shelves or bins for pamphlets, glassware or packaging.

Above the shelves the supergraphics called out quietly for attention. Millet explained the graphics he had in mind to Michael Manwaring and Gerald Reis, of San Francisco, who made 8" by 10" pencil drawings of seeds, a beet leaf, a lobster, asparagus stalks, etc. Millet had these converted into 8" by 10" mezzotints, then enlarged to 12' by 6' negatives. Using full-sized silk screens, workmen, with understandable difficulty, screened the graphics in place. Most of the graphics used three colors, some four. Manwaring and Reis went to the trouble of silk-screening because they wanted the shadings and the dotted effect.

Beyond this array of products and packages, "we wanted to show the retailer how to display our merchandise," says Millet. So he hired what he calls a "stylist," a display designer, who produced several possible store settings using different Corning products.

These trade shows have become something Millet handles while still involved in the usual range of Corning design projects. He fit this one into four months and a $75,000 budget.

Client: Corning Glassworks
Design firm: Corning Design, Corning, NY
Designer: Gerald Millet
Graphic consultants: Michael Manwaring, Gerald Reis
Fabricator: Warren Display Co.

3. Supergraphics were silk-screened with full-sized screens.
4. Cabinets, some hanging from the ceiling grid, are of painted birch.

Exhibition Design/22

New, Drip, Serve and Drink coffee
Pyrex Ware and Corning Ware Products

Design Education at Pratt Institute

Education at Pratt Institute in Brooklyn is increasingly interdisciplinary. Students there can take courses freely in any of three departments: Interior Design, Industrial Design and Graphics. It is an approach suited to work in most of today's design offices. The successful private offices are usually flexible and multi-faceted, taking on work in graphics and product design, exhibits or interiors. If a designer wants to specialize in, say, products, he will join the staff of a General Motors or a John Deere.

Pratt gave Etan Manasse Associates the task of presenting this interdisciplinary facet of Pratt's design philosophy in the ground-floor exhibit gallery of New York's Lever House. Manasse, who besides running his own office is chairman of Pratt's visual communications department, wanted a display device that would contrast with Lever House's formal, straight-lined, hard-edged steel and glass. The Lever Gallery has glass walls on three sides, one facing park Avenue and its constant pedestrian and vehicular traffic. So Manasse, further, wanted something that would catch the eyes of passersby, something that "looked good from the sidewalk."

In his office, Manasse fashioned a quarter-scale model of the Lever House exhibition space; also to scale, he built—by cutting and joining core paneled doors—four cubes with top surfaces large enough to hold several items for display. "Our concept," says Manasse, "defied the traditional exhibit method of displaying each object on a separate pedestal." He went further, giving the upper surfaces of these cubes an undulating look, what he calls an "organic or sand-dune effect," to contrast with the glass box of Lever House and its exhibit gallery. "I walked by the exhibit one day while it was snowing and it looked as if the snow had made the shapes on our display surfaces," says Manasse. This organic look was achieved in the final installation by scattering cardboard half-domes randomly on top of the cubes, covering both domes and cube tops with foam-rubber sheets to produce a smooth overall surface, and cloaking the foam rubber with stretch fabric.

Amidst the undulations of these four surfaces, which were 7′ by 9′ square and 40″

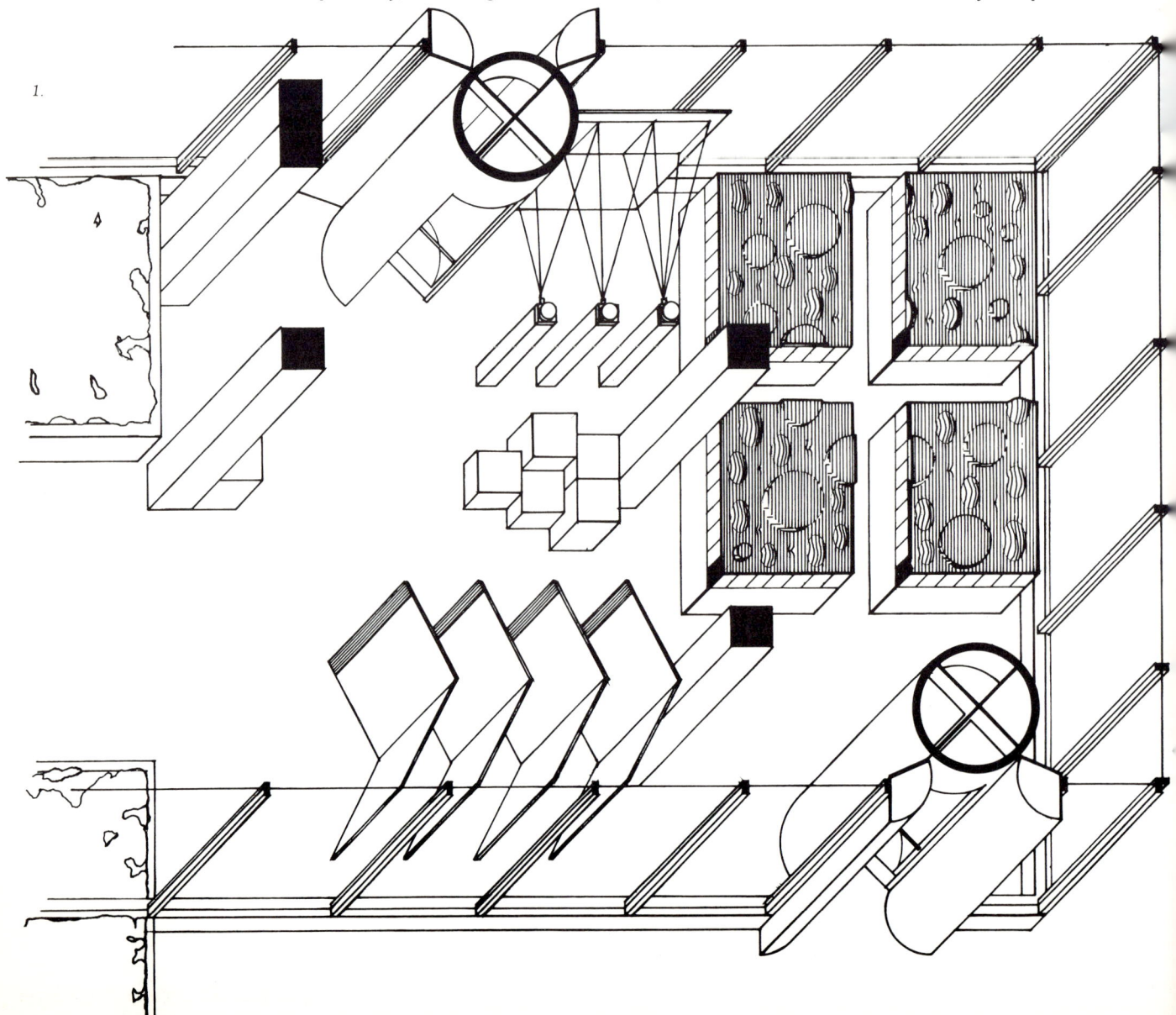

1.

off the floor, Manasse placed students' three-dimensional prototype designs for such things as a voice writer, a video phone, a prefabricated bathroom, a line of porcelain dinnerware based on traditional Thai designs, a "push-swing non-motorized vehicle" and a modular structural system of paper. Packaging and graphics were mixed with the products, though two-dimensional graphics were hung on free-standing 4' by 8' surfaces elsewhere in the exhibit space; a slide presentation on three 4' by 5½' screens showed still more student work. Items in

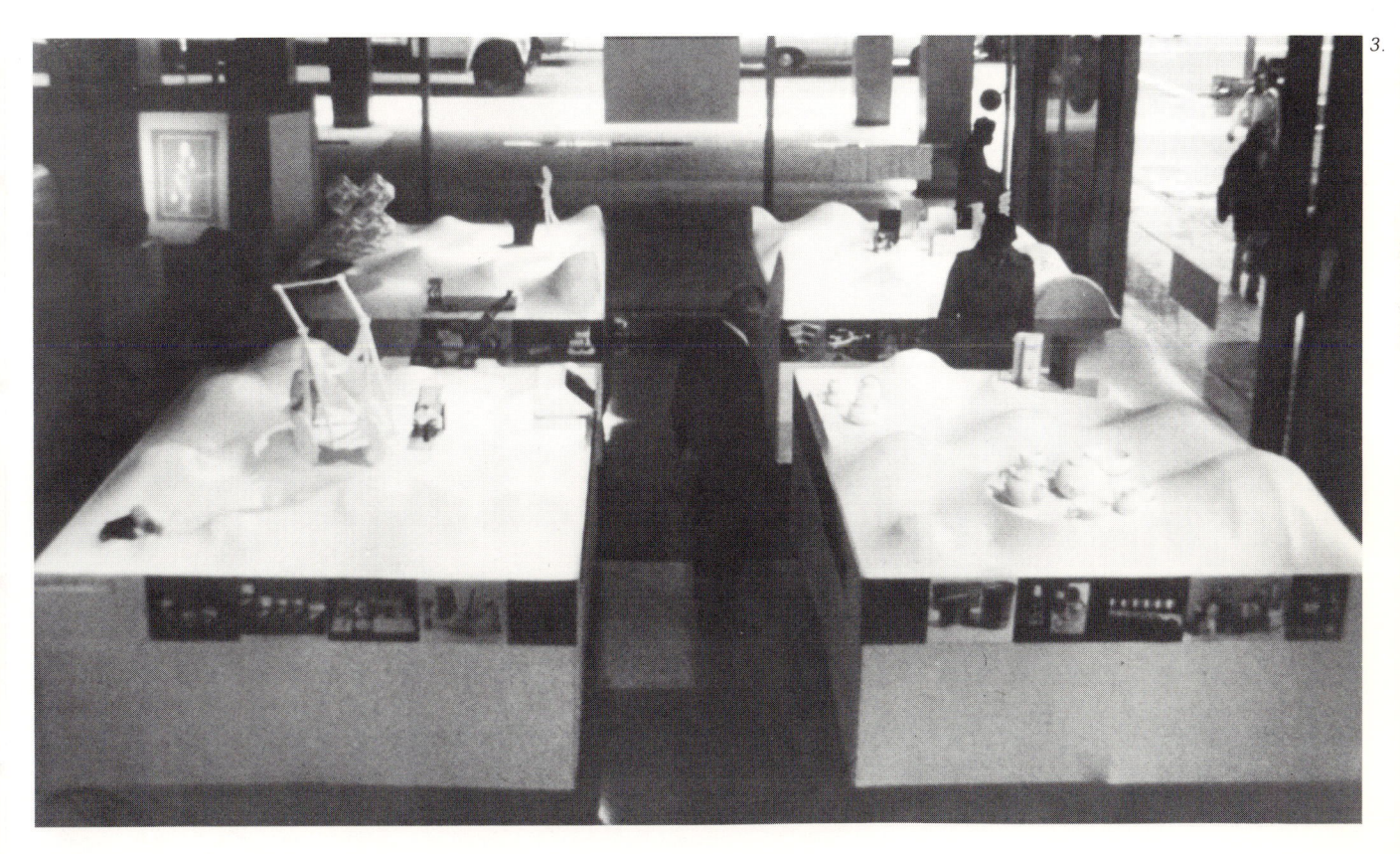

1. Floor plan.
2. Mailing piece announcing Pratt exhibit.
3. Lever House exhibit space opens on Park Avenue.

25/Exhibition Design

the exhibit were numbered and visitors given a guide sheet, naming each artifact. Type was little used, but where it did show up it was a Futura Light, which Manasse considers complementary to the form and dimension of the display structures.

Visitors could identify which department had produced which work through a color code. Graduate work was marked by a darker shade of the color used for a particular department's undergraduate work.

Manasse produced the exhibit on a budget of $4500, using unsalaried student help.

Client: Pratt Institute (Brooklyn, NY)
Design firm: Etan Manasse Associates, Inc., New York
Designers: Etan Manasse, Steven Lee, David Freedman, Elisabeth Levine
Fabricators: Jeff Hannigan and students in Pratt's work-study program.

4. Student pottery design.
5. Push-swing non-motorized vehicle.

Exhibition Design/26

Living History Center

You walk to your seat, down into the 875-seat theater. In front of you is the world's largest movie screen, almost seven stories high and nine stories wide. As the lights dim, you hear galloping hoofbeats behind you, then straining muscle and leather as horse and rider leap over you onto the 70' by 93' screen to announce the start of the American Revolution. IMAX is the process Francis Thompson used to photograph his 48-minute sweep through American history. His film is one of 29 audio-visual events in Philadelphia's Living History Center.

Ralph Appelbaum, who designed the Center's exhibit with Murry Gelberg, as consultants to Raymond Loewy International, says it is the first attempt to do an exhibit entirely with audio-visual equipment. The attempt is, of course, controversial, for not everyone is ready for an exhibit without artifacts and with an absolute minimum of accompanying text. Even traffic flow is accomplished without signs. The flow is random, visitors moving from one exhibit area to another in sequences dictated by whim or fancy, not by design.

Appelbaum and Gelberg had an exhibit budget of $1.65 million and 16,000 sq. ft. to work with, and they filled the space almost entirely with audio-visual presentations. Using a Unistrut system with a custom aluminum skeleton onto which they snapped 28"-square Formica panels, they created surfaces, spaces and even rooms in which the slide projectors, microfilm readouts, quiz machines, audio headsets,

1.

1. Watching a 6-minute film on American inventions.

video playback monitors and motion picture projectors operate. There are, for instance, 19 mini-theaters. "We chose simple equipment and tried to put it together in a unique way," says Appelbaum.

As you descend from the IMAX theater onto a deck you see the exhibit hall beneath you. "We designed the exhibit to look dramatic from that view," Appelbaum explains. Everything is in 28" modules, mostly blocks of the Formica-covered Unistrut.

These blocks echo the block-like steps, which form the roof of the IMAX theater. Though the building was new when Loewy International was asked to design the exhibit, there was no coordination between the architects, Mitchell/Giurgola Associates, and the Loewy designers. Appelbaum and Gelberg were merely shown the completed space (on Philadelphia's Independence Mall) and asked to fill it with a self-supporting exhibit, "celebrating the American experience." It was to be the country's premier Bicentennial exhibit and toward that end, Philadelphia '76, Inc. (Philadelphia's Bicentennial agency) put up $11.5 million. Most of that went for the building, which includes a couple of restaurants, a playground, a gift shop, in addition to the exhibits.

Punctuating the masses of modular blocks on the exhibit floor are 10 cylindrical columns, hanging from the exposed-truss 20' ceiling to 28" above the floor. Peering at visitors from the lower end of each vinyl-clad fiberglass

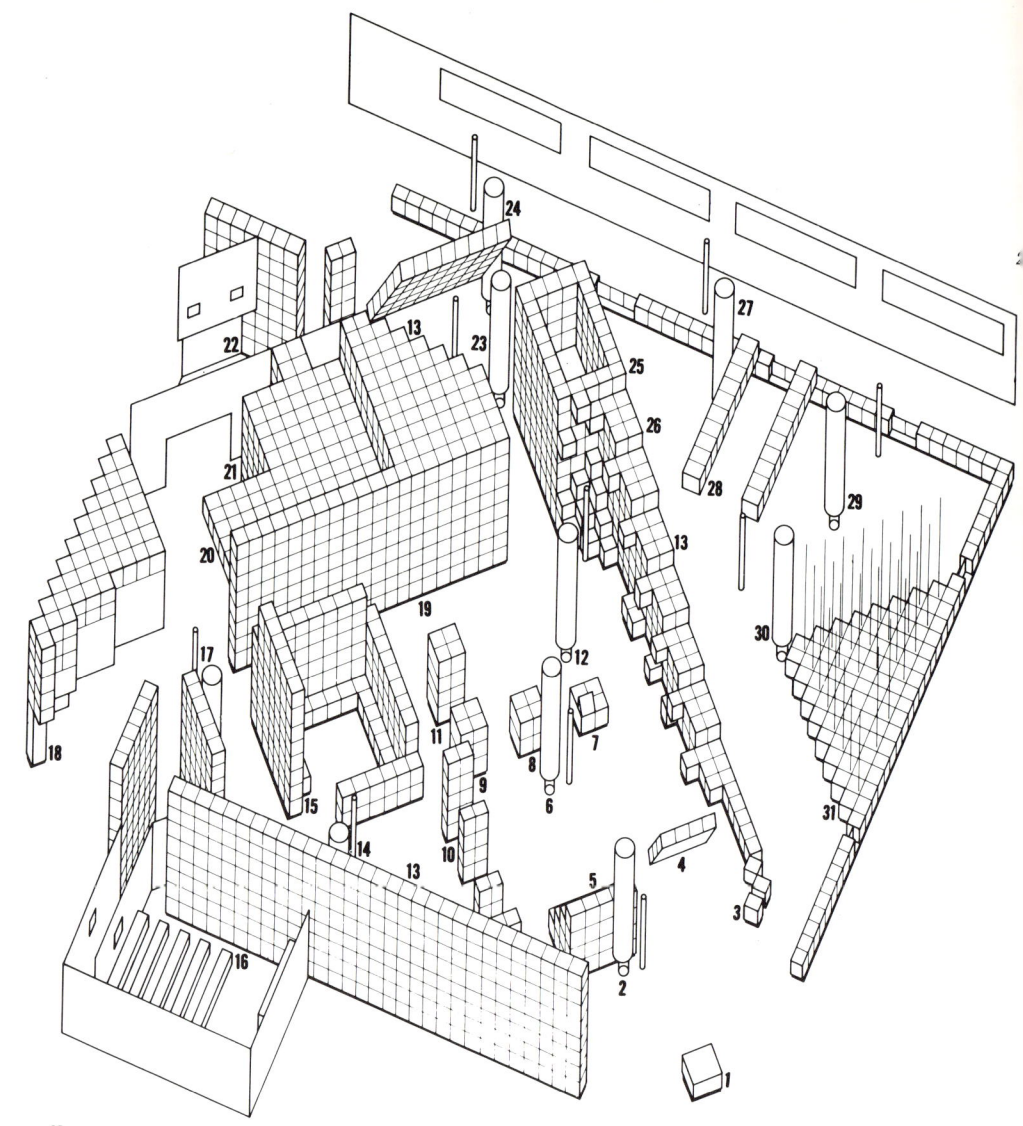

Key:
1. Directory
2. Film: America
3. Timeline
4. Slide show: Flags
5. Nine flip book albums
6. Film: Women
7. Memory bank typewriter
8. Multiple-choice question-answer machines
9. Microfilm storage and readout
10. Eight stereo headsets: One-minute comedy routines
11. Two stereopticon viewers
12. Film: Presidents
13. Forty-one stereo headsets: Soundscapes
14. Film: Freedom
15. Rotating trylons: Cities
16. Film: To Secure These Rights
17. Film: Portraits
18. Interlocking slide projectors (six) and film projector (one): Crafts
19. Sixty-four slide projectors with faders: To the New World
20. Twelve color video monitors on overhead track: Assembly Line
21. Film projector in mirrored room: Songbook
22. Two custom crawl projectors: Sports
23. Video monitor: Newsreels
24. Video monitor: Religion
25. Interlocking slide projectors (two) and film projector (one): Future
26. Multiple-choice question-and-answer readout: Vote
27. Video monitor: Indians
28. Six slide projectors: Landscapes
29. Video monitor: Pioneers
30. Video monitor: Inventiveness
31. Photo panel structure: Inventions

Exhibition Design/28

2. Floor plan.
3. Child with headset.
4-6. Exhibit in use.

29/Exhibition Design

cylinder is a TV set. Each provides, at the push of a button, a six-minute film on bits of the American experience—pioneers, Indians, freedom, etc. All 10 films (one for each TV set) originate by closed circuit from a central control room, which contains the equipment needed to produce the entire exhibit's sounds and images. One man can handle the equipment.

Though the technology seems complex, the designers planned ahead to thwart the mechanical problems that plague so many audio-visual displays. The Center has a permanent repairman, trained by the equipment suppliers, who breaks down and services at regular intervals the Center's 80 slide projectors, six motion picture projectors, 22 videotape playback monitors, the closed-circuit video system, and assorted other machinery. Moreover, some of the equipment is selected to be self-maintaining. Slide projectors, for instance, are all equipped with six bulbs and a system that snaps a fresh bulb into place as a used one expires. All the exhibit modules have removable panels, so the maintenance man can easily take the equipment out for repair; and the designers specified a separate work-light system for use when the Center is closed. A sampling of the Center's exhibit:

• A 64-projector slide show on a single 20′ by 20′ screen. Produced around the theme "My Father Was an Immigrant," the show consists of single images, sections of which are thrown on 28″-square segments of the giant screen by all 64 projectors. These images are of areas of the U.S., e.g., its southeastern swamps. Then, within this single image, individual 28″ images, faces, begin to appear, dotted throughout the scene.

• A giant stereopticon machine, whose slides move on an internal belt. You look through an eyepiece and watch the slides flip by. A lower eyepiece is for children. Slides, from the Library of Congress, show such things as scenes of the San Francisco earthquake, the Klondike Gold Rush, the Civil War.

• Fifty stereo earphones, suspended on flexible wires, each carry a separate one-minute audio vignette... Mark Twain talking about the blue jay, for instance, or a voice describing the start of the Oklahoma land rush.

• A tiny kaleidoscope theater, 14′ wide and 7′ high, with mirrored floor and ceiling, in which are played American songs from ballad to rock, accompanied by projected images. Sample: "You Ain't Nothin' But a Hound Dog" with reflected slides of Elvis Presley and a hound.

• A 15-minute dramatic film on the Bill of Rights.

• A 70′-long History Walk, using cube-mounted photos and brief 150-word texts to give a quick survey of American historical highlights.

The history presented throughout the exhibit is fragmented. But even so, the Center bombards one's senses so continually that one must leave and return in order to take in the entire exhibit. It is too much to ingest, or to stand, in one visit.

7. Looking from the Inventions section toward the beginning of the exhibit.

Client: Philadelphia '76, Inc.
Design firm: Raymond Loewy International
Consultant designers: Ralph Appelbaum (project director), Murry Gelberg
Other consultants: Lynch Industries; Bergen Expo Systems; Imero Fiorentino Associates; Nancy Hechinger
Fabricator: Lynch Exhibits

Exhibition Design/30

MAN transFORMS

Carrying the banner of the Smithsonian Institution, the Cooper-Hewitt Museum reopened in the fall of 1976 as the national museum of design. Its quarters are in what was once Andrew Carnegie's New York house and garden at 91st Street and Fifth Avenue. As a national museum of design it might have been expected to open its doors with a splashy exhibit of the current "best" in American design. But the exhibit greeting visitors was current only in the broadest sense and more international than American. On a basic level, of course, design has no boundaries, and Hans Hollein, the Austrian architect-designer whom the Cooper-Hewitt asked to put together its opening show, wanted to avoid judgments about good design and to avoid an easy display of designers' work. His guidelines were broad: the museum wanted an exhibit that would "give the public an understanding of the word 'design' and how it affects our lives." Whatever else "MAN transFORMS/Aspects of Design" accomplished, it was a remarkable amalgam of individual design talent, government institutional guidance and private corporate capital. The exhibit's $600,000 budget came entirely from the Johnson Wax Company. As the Cooper-Hewitt's director, Lisa Taylor, points out in a forward to the exhibit catalogue, "It required patience and courage to support a *new* institution and exhibition when both were in their earliest conceptual stage."

Hollein gathered an

1. Structure in nature and man-made design follow the same mathematical laws.
2. Smithsonian Institution's National Museum of Design was once Andrew Carnegie's New York mansion. This rendering of house appears on Cooper-Hewitt letterhead.

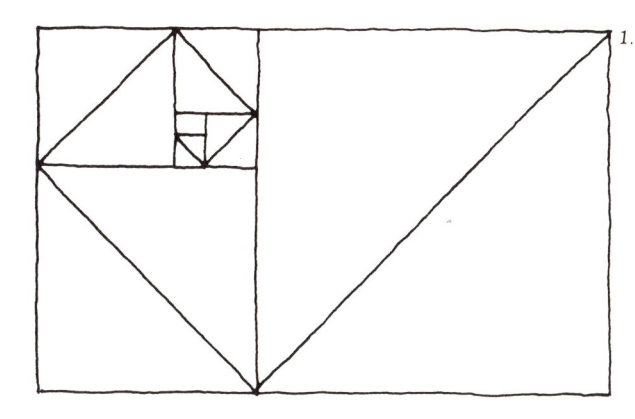

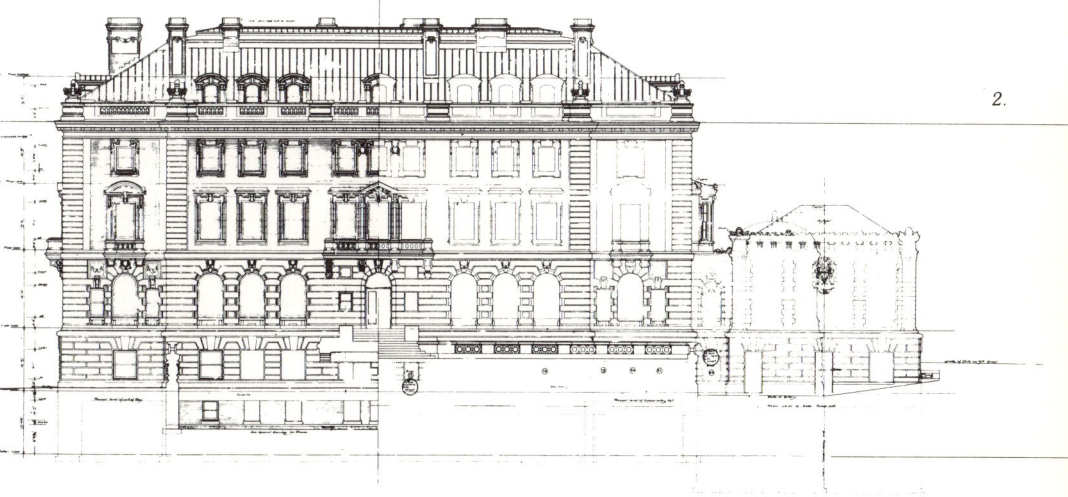

31/Exhibition Design

international team of architects and designers, asking each to contribute an exhibit. Two, Richard Meier and R. Buckminster Fuller, are Americans. The others were: Ettore Sottsass (Italy), Peter M. Bode (Germany), Murray Grigor (Scotland), Oswald Mattias Ungers (Germany), Arata Isozaki (Japan), Nader Ardalan and Karl Schlamminger (Iran). The complexities generated by designers putting together an exhibit from such disparate nooks of the world is easily imagined. Even the designers who happened to be in New York faced complications. They could make no on-site studies because the exhibit areas were being renovated and transformed.

The Casebook jurors liked the exhibit setting in an old mansion, and they praised the variety with which the designers displayed textures, shapes and colors, producing what the jurors called a "total exhibit," one with something for everyone, an exhibit that was tactile and participatory. Sometimes that audience participation differed from what the designers intended. Children, for instance, more often used Richard Meier's "Metamorphosis" (constructed with an Abstracta system) as a jungle gym rather than as a structure for a word game.

Briefly, this is what each designer contributed:

Hans Hollein, to illustrate the endless proliferation of designs possible with a single material, collected examples of man's restless tampering with a piece of cloth. It becomes a ribbon, a banner, clothing, shelter, a gag, a bandage, "an infinity of forms" and textures. "Man invariably feels challenged by plain surfaces and adds line, color, pattern to create symbolic and decorative embellishments," says Hollein. On wood frames 4'-square, Hollein stretched cloth squares containing decorative embellishments. In combinations of four or more he laid these squares flat to form a table of patterns, propped them upright to form a wall or partition, and even leaned them jauntily against a wall. He set up in the exhibit a tepee, a Bedouin tent, a cloth windmill from Greece, a cloth-wrapped airplane and a kite. Banners and saris are cloth, Hollein reminds us, and so are sails, balloons and umbrellas. On exhibit, borrowed from another Smithsonian collection, was the world's largest ship in a bottle, 18' long, including the cork, a ship put together with 14 different types of sails.

Elsewhere, to illustrate the variety of shapes and textures achieved with a single material, Hollein covered a wooden table with bread as it is prepared in different cultures, breads as buns, discs, crescents, stars, loaves. And conversely, to illustrate the materials and textures of a single shape, Hollein collected stars, hanging them beneath a 12'-high blue-felt dome: starfish, jewels, Christmas tree ornaments, a chandelier, sheriff badges, glass stars, tin stars, gold stars, cloth stars. He also set up a procession of doors, as if seen in endless mirrors, as well as a display of hammers.

Peter M. Bode filled a wall with handles and opening devices—knobs, faucets, fasteners.

O. M. Ungers juxtaposed photos of city plans with photos of unexpectedly corresponding natural shapes ... the city plan as cross, as a man-made earth satellite, as a star, as a freshly blooming rose.

Arata Isozaki set up an exhibit of cages. One, 8' high, was formed by setting a quarter section of a brass rod cage in the corner of a mirrored room. In the cage, against the mirror, was one-quarter of a papier-mâché reproduction of an angel in Fra Angelico's painting, "Annunciation."

Nader Ardalan and Karl Schlamminger created a sacred room of 34" plexiglass squares. They threaded these on four steel rods, gradually stepping these squares as they built from the floor to create an arched, peaked structure 11½' high. It was shaped like traditional Persian architectural design, with the space beneath lighted by a spotlight shining through a hole at the top and reflecting through the plexiglass pieces.

Murray Grigor contributed ten short films on such subjects as automobile design, faces, oasis and dressing.

Ettore Sottsass displayed photographs of real designs, for example an Olivetti typewriter, and of fanciful designs, such as a highway between two anthills and a television for night butterflies.

Richard Meier constructed a labyrinthine structure of 1' Abstracta sections bolted in a framework 10' wide and 9'4" high. Within the open squares

Exhibition Design/32

3. "City Metaphors" by O. M. Ungers.
4. Richard Meier's word grid.
5. Hans Hollein's "Stars."
6. Arata Isozaki's "Cages."

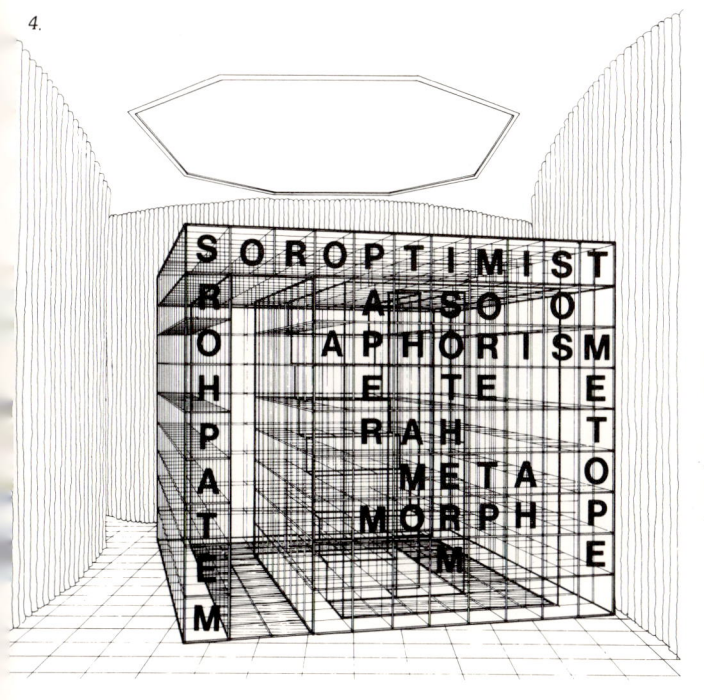

33/Exhibition Design

of the space-grid framework he clipped cards carrying letters from the word "metamorphosis." It became a word game in which he urged visitors to participate by taking cards and clipping them to the framework, spelling out words in three dimensions.

R. Buckminster Fuller contributed a film scenario for the universe, in which he identifies the universe's building blocks. He uses some of them in constructing his geodesic domes.

Unanimous in their praise of "MAN transFORMS," the Casebook jurors called it a study in human excellence. Visitors to the exhibit were also impressed. Said a Cooper-Hewitt spokesman: "While the press reactions were mixed and often reflected an inability to deal with the show, the public response was very positive and enthusiastic. Many visitors came back two and three times."

Client: Cooper-Hewitt Museum (New York), the Smithsonian Institution's National Museum of Design
Design firm: Hans Hollein, Vienna
Designers: Hans Hollein, R. Buckminster Fuller, Ettore Sottsass, Peter M. Bode, Richard Meier, Murray Grigor, Oswald Mattias Ungers, Arata Isozaki, Nader Ardalan, Karl Schlamminger
Consultants: George Nelson (catalog), Dorothy Twining Globus, David Lerner, Lucy Fellowes
Fabricators: CDI; Spaeth Displays

7. Hans Hollein's "Bread."
8. Hans Hollein's "Metamorphosis of a Square of Cloth."
9. Arata Isozaki's "Angel Cage."

History of Rocketry and Space Flight

Gallery 113 at the Smithsonian Institution's National Air and Space Museum holds an exhibit on the history of rocketry and space flight. Space flight has been a matter of fantasy for more years than it's been a matter of fact, and the exhibit put together by Herbst/La Zar Design and the NASM staff recognizes both elements.

Visitors entering the 6000-sq. ft. gallery with its 16′ ceiling pass a brief two-screen slide show in which photos of science-fiction magazine covers flash in sequence with actual space events. "This is meant to get visitors in the proper mood for the exhibit," says Tom D. Crouch, NASM associate curator for astronautics, who borrowed a Buck Rogers rocket pistol and a solar scout badge from his father, H. D. Crouch, for display in the exhibit.

Divided into three sections, the exhibit treats fantasy, history and rocket engines (with a brief concluding section speculating on future propulsion systems). Herbst/La Zar help maintain distinctions by grading the colors used from soft to strong, using muted blues and violets, for instance, in the fantasy section, then letting the colors get progressively stronger until in the rocket engine displays the colors are bold reds, yellows and greens. Also, the typeface changes from Optima in the fantasy and history sections to Outline Helvetica among the rocket engines.

As might be expected, some of the rocket engines are massive. The engine from a Titan rocket, for example, is

1, 2. Future rockets and propulsion systems.

1.

2.

16' long, but the National Air and Space Museum, which has, among other artifacts, a DC-3 hanging from its rafters, was built to take large internal loads. Gallery 113 is no exception, and rocket engines hang from the ceiling and stand on the floor. In almost every instance an engine is accompanied by a photo blowup or a silk-screening of the rocket it was designed to power. Graphics appear everywhere, on the back (or front) of exhibit pedestals, on partitions, and on panels suspended from the ceiling. Though the Casebook jurors thought the graphics sometimes cluttered, and were not overwhelmed by the quality of the supergraphic cartoon murals, they praised the exhibit's organization and its richness.

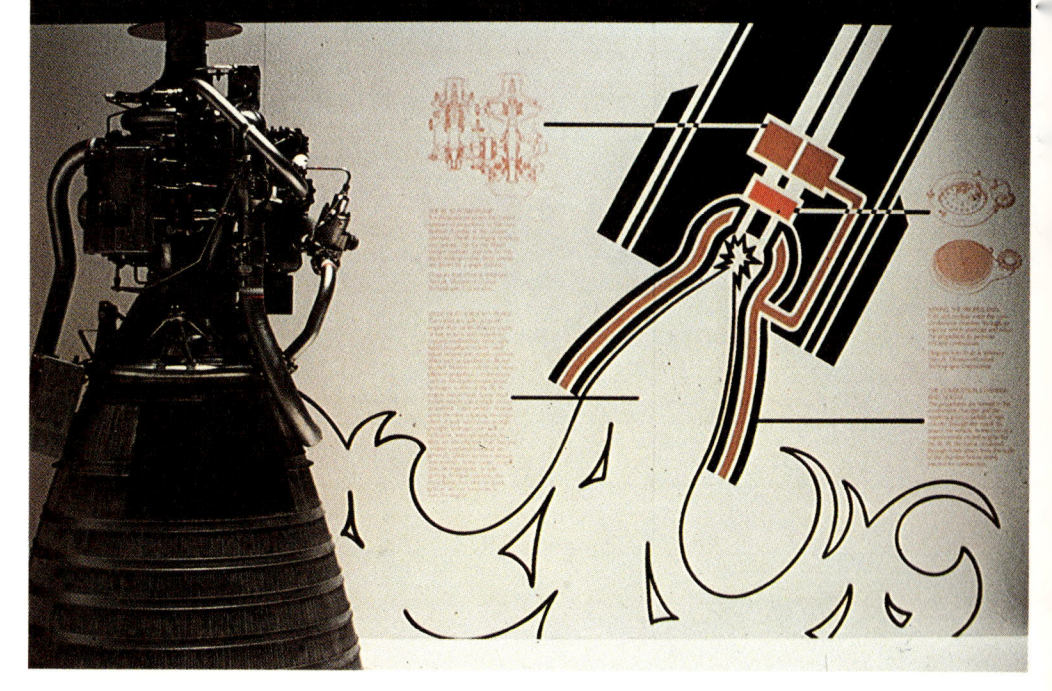

Client: National Air and Space Museum, Smithsonian Institution (Washington, D.C.)
Design firm: Herbst/LaZar Design, Inc., Chicago
Designers: Ralph LaZar, Randall Bell, Mellissa Woodburn, Jay Tinen
Fabricator: Lynch Industries

3. An illustration of Newton's second law.
4. Rocket engine and diagram.

Exhibition Design/36

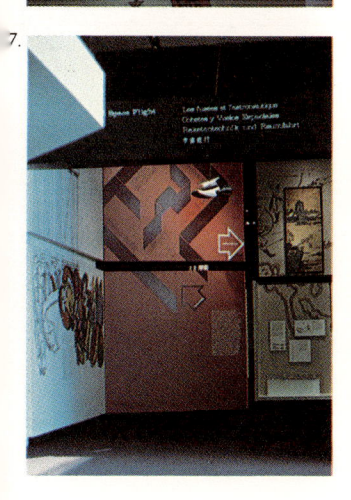

5-9. Graphics enliven exhibit.

37/Exhibition Design

Graphic Communications Student Show

Assigned to produce a student show, graduate students Michael J. Toti and Mike Whitney, of Washington University's Graphic Communications Department, started from scratch. They knew only that the exhibit space measured 20′ by 70′ by 8′ and that they had $800 to work with. Their involvement was perhaps more personal than that of most exhibit designers in most shows, for the purpose of this exhibit—to give viewers a better understanding of what graphic communication students do—provided Whitney and Toti with a chance to state their own case. To work with, they had the best Washington University student design efforts of the year.

Their organization was logical (by class) and their exhibit device simple—a series of eight-sided, corrugated cardboard modules, stapled together, which served as space dividers, exhibition surfaces and housings for rear-projected slide presentations.

Arranged to divide the exhibit equitably, a 7′-high module introduced each class's space; in addition, one module stood at the entrance, heralding the show. Hand-painted with outdoor poster colors on the front surfaces of these modules were historical graphic representations. Introducing the show, for instance, was a mural representing the cave paintings from Lascaux. Just above this mural, along the module's top edge, ran Normandie Italic letters, cut from a 6-ply Strathmore board, raised a quarter inch from the surface by balsa pieces, spelling out "Graphic Communications." Whitney and Toti picked Normandie Italic to soften, with its rounded lines, the modules' rectilinearity.

They wanted each introductory mural to represent a milestone in the history of graphic communication. The

1.

Lascaux paintings are, of course, the earliest graphic arts still extant. The Bayeaux Tapestry (a representation of which introduced the sophomore section) is sometimes considered a foreshadowing of the contemporary comic strip. A Toulouse-Lautrec poster (juniors) commemorated one of the earliest illustrator-designers. And a mural of characters from the Beatles' *Yellow Submarine,* an animation classic, introduced the seniors and graduate students.

Within this historical context, say Toti and Whitney, "the viewer was asked to judge the efforts of Washington University students in their attempts to solve graphic communications problems." The two designers selected what they considered the best work for display, either hanging it on walls or modules or placing it on the modules' flat-topped surfaces. Each item was accompanied by a text (in "American typewriter"). And they supplemented displayed work with slide presentations, showing still more examples from each class.

Toti and Whitney designed, organized, fabricated and supervised the show's installation. Preparatory work took most of a month.

1. Exhibit entrance
2. Detail of sophomore section introduction
3. Senior and graduate student section
4. Detail of junior section introduction

Installation took three days. Though the client in this case was the Graphic Communications Department and final approval was up to department heads, the students worked (with faculty advisor-consultants) essentially on their own. In fact, one consultant was a student—James Olvera, a junior, who helped develop a multi-mirrored rear-screen projector unit. And Toti and Whitney found satisfaction in seeing their exhibit designed and installed quickly, without what they call "the usual client alterations and reworking of ideas."

OBJECTIVE: To design an annual report and cover for Washington University's School of Fine Arts which conveys an image of the school, using a grid structure.

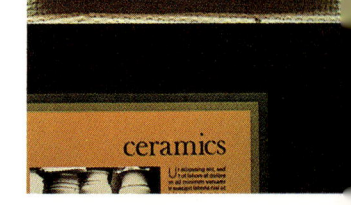

Client: Graphic Communications Department, Washington University (St. Louis, MO)
Designers: Michael J. Toti, Mike Whitney
Consultants: James Olvera, David Borella, Richard Brunell, Ted Smith, Gene Hoefel
Fabricators: Michael J. Toti, Mike Whitney, Ray Brouck

5. View through exhibit area.
6. Plan.
7. Statement of purpose.

Saga of the Great Plains

"I am a Western buff and this was my topic," says John Vorhes in speaking of his involvement with the International Communication Agency's traveling exhibit, "The Saga of the Great Plains." Vorhes was the ICA staff designer in charge of the exhibit, and his enthusiasm rubbed off on the rest of his team. "Those who weren't previously Western buffs are now hooked," he claims.

Probably what helped congeal everyone's enthusiasm was the tight time schedule. Normally, Vorhes and his staff would have had five months to design, fabricate, and gather artifacts for the $46,000 exhibit. But because of the way ICA's fiscal budget is set up, Vorhes had to have his research, his design concept and construction contract completed in less than two months. If he didn't, funds for the project couldn't be allocated. Then, four months after the award of the construction contract, fabrication had to be completed, artifacts assembled and the exhibit on its way to Melbourne, Australia, its first Far Eastern installation.

But if the constantly imminent deadlines and the close cooperation needed to meet them produced exhilaration, it is possible that more time would have helped the exhibit. Vorhes is convinced, for instance, that a search for lighter materials could have reduced the shipping weight from 3500 pounds.

James Hargrove, Ambassador to Australia, and a Texan, came up with the exhibit idea. Struck by the

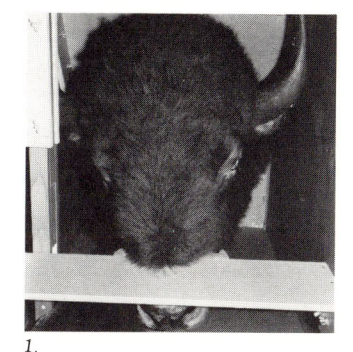

1.

2.

1. Buffalo head packed for shipment to Australia.
2. Over 1½ tons of exhibit, packed mostly in 34" cubes of molded polyethelene, arrive in Melbourne.
3. Plan.

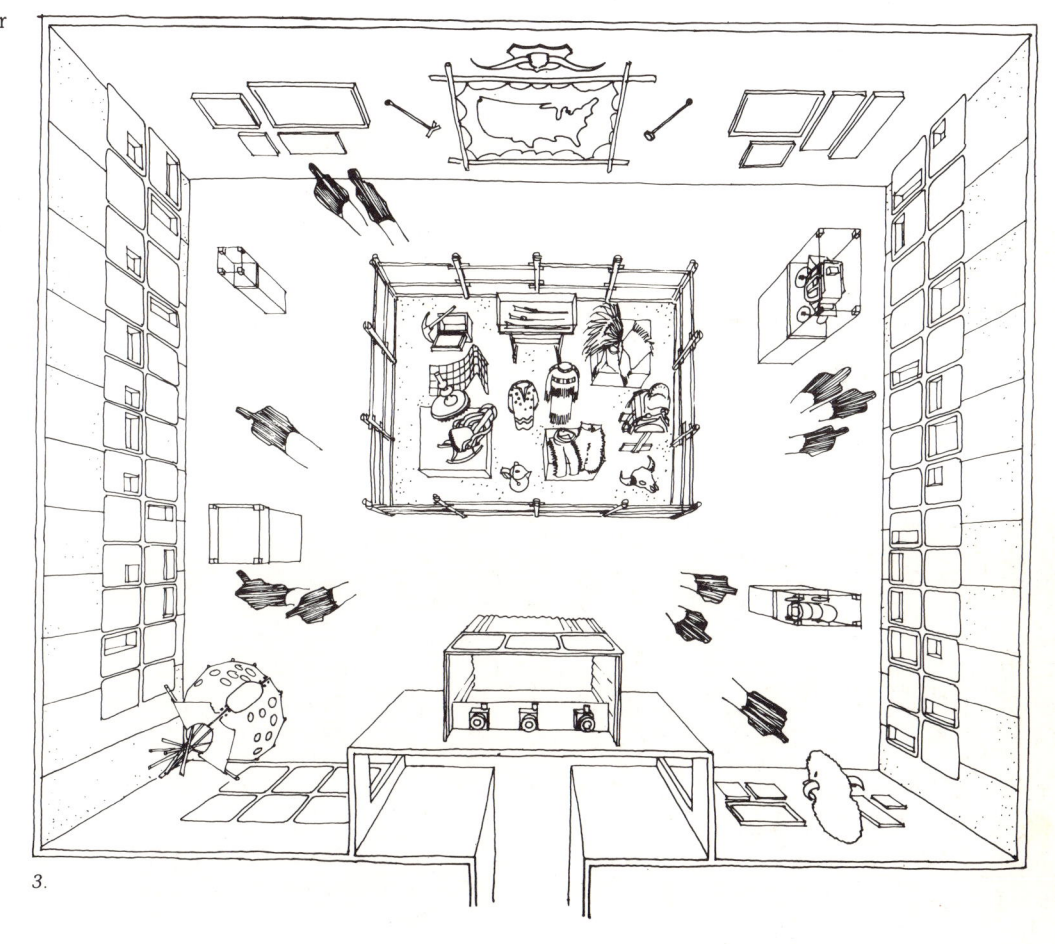

3.

41/Exhibition Design

similarities between America's westward expansion and the settlement of Australia's outback, Hargrove thought an exhibit highlighting these parallels would fit in with the ICA's Australian program. The Agency, knowing how the American West ignites imaginations throughout the Far East, agreed, but wanted to widen the exhibit's influence by shipping it (after Australia) to New Zealand, the Philippines, New Guinea and Thailand.

Once the assignment became definite, Vorhes traveled west from Washington, D.C., visiting state historical societies and museums. Their support was immediate; and artifacts such as a stuffed buffalo head, a Texas Ranger's knife inscribed "Hurrah for Hell," a Blackfoot tepee, Pony Express horseshoes and saddle bag, a steer-horn rocking chair, a beer bottle from Judge Roy Bean's saloon, a battered bugle found after the battle of Little Big Horn, began accumulating in Washington.

It soon became apparent that an exhibit on the entire West was too unwieldy. So, explains Vorhes, "we limited ourselves to the story of the Great Plains from about 1865 to the turn of the century." These were the years of the cowboys and Indians, sod busters and railroads, wagon trains of settlers, the Pony Express and stage coaches... what people think of when they think of the Wild West.

Though the subject was defined, Vorhes and his colleagues still had no idea where the exhibit might be hung, and they could only proceed by anticipating the worst possible Far Eastern conditions. (Actually, the exhibit was booked into some very elegant surroundings, such as the Sydney Opera House.)

The system they came up with is a 33"-square Masonite panel, into which an 8"-deep display case lined with suede cloth can be dropped. Designed in various sizes, these boxes can take up an entire panel or be much smaller, just large enough, say, to hold a pair of beadwork moccasins or boxes and bottles from a frontier community general store. These handsome panels, each with its own lighting, were wall-hung with simple reveals between them. Graphics and text were screened onto each panel's surface. For background Vorhes used a sand color—appropriate for the Great Plains—with brown lettering, Souvenir for texts and West Behemoth for headlines, because, though contemporary, it has a "slight Western flair." Each panel was meant to be self-contained so that installers could mount them in patterns determined at each site.

Boxes and panels were separated for shipment in the 34" cubes of polyethylene airline containers.

When set into the panels, the plexiglass-covered display cases provided their own security. Seemingly less secure were the sawdust-covered floor areas cordoned off by an approximation of a Western rail fence. The Casebook jurors found these areas, which displayed more artifacts —dolls, furniture, buffalo robes, clothing—often on uncovered pedestals, "daring in this kind of show." Their security, it turned out, was more real than apparent. Artifacts were set back at least a meter from the rail fence, and the fence itself, though flimsy, acted as an effective barrier. "People would touch the fence," explains Vorhes, who had not planned things this way, "see how flimsy it was (it would move beneath their hands), and would quickly move back." Moreover, there was almost always a guard or a guide in the exhibit area to keep watch. Nor were these railed areas as difficult to set up as they might seem. ICA sent out a catalogue with the exhibit that showed color photographs of the fenced areas with diagrams and text explaining exactly how to set it up and where to position lights. Each ICA post provided sawdust for the floor.

The exhibit contained a third, more traditional display device—plexiglass cases, which held artifacts atop burlap-covered pedestals. These unbolted for shipping.

In a year-long trip through the Far East, "The Saga of the Great Plains" was uncrated and set up in nine cities, including Kuala Lumpur and Port Moresby, where viewers found that their conception of the American West, formed mostly by Hollywood, was largely myth. "Our educated visitors," says Vorhes, "were pleased by our honest approach to the suffering and defeat of the American Indian."

Vorhes found the project exhilarating beyond its subject and his staff's empathy. "It was particularly satisfying to work with the various museum curators involved, who knew their subject so well and had great respect for the artifacts in their collections."

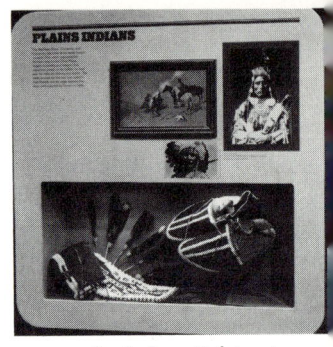

Client: International Communication Agency (formerly USIA; Washington, D.C.)
Design firm: ICA Exhibit Design Staff, Washington, D.C.
Designers: John Vorhes, Ethel Freid
Consultants: Edward Hunter (research and writing), Roy Anderson (illustrator), Linda Hicks, Sandra Shank
Fabricator: William P. Gelberg

Exhibition Design/42

4, 5. Display cases set in Masonite panels.
6, 7. Exhibit hung in Manilla. Display case in foreground holds artifacts from Battle of Little Big Horn.
8. Exhibit set up in National Museum of Art, Port Moresby, New Guinea.
9. Artifacts corralled in AMP building lobby, Melbourne.
10. Specially remodeled hall in the Museum of South Australia, Adelaide.
11. Though fence is flimsy, vandalism is discouraged by placing displays well back from fence.

43/Exhibition Design

Greek Pavilion

Though a Montreal architectural firm—Dimitri, Dimakopoulos—was responsible along with Jacques Guillon/Designers for the exhibit in the Greek Pavilion at "Man and His World 1976," there was no architecture involved. Site for the exhibit, which besides promoting Greek trade and industry provided a historic review of the Greek Olympics, coinciding with the contemporary Olympic games held in Montreal that summer, was the former Belgian pavilion on the Expo '67 fairgrounds. The pavilion had bright colors and lots of glass to bring in washes of outside light. What the designers wanted from the Greek exhibit was a building subdued in color, depending entirely on interior lighting. "We couldn't have outside light," says Laurent Marquart, the partner-in-charge for Jacques Guillon/Designers. "All the mystery would be destroyed by natural light."

So, though they left the Belgian red brick untouched on some walls, they painted other walls and ceiling dark blue (blues appear throughout to coincide with Greek blue) and covered the extensive windows with sheet rock. Inside, ceiling spotlights pinpointed everything—statues, photomurals, and triangular exhibit bins and platforms. These latter showcases were modular, either 8' or 3½' on a side. Constructed of wood and glass, they formed platforms for sculptures, surfaces for silk-screened graphics or (when topped by glass boxes) cases in which smaller artifacts

1. Case holds ancient and modern Olympic artifacts.
2. Plaster reproduction of statue of Olympic athletes.
3. Triangular structures become bins, platforms, and, cut on a bias, surfaces for graphics.

Exhibition Design/44

45/Exhibition Design

could be displayed.

The exhibit consisted of three distinct areas: 1) Olympic Games; 2) historic Greece; 3) modern Greece. A partition system provided backdrops and channeled people through the pavilion. Overhead canvas banners identified areas and specific objects (e.g., Zeus, God of Gods). "We wanted to show the influence history has on life in modern Greece," says Laurent Marquart; "the tradition of handicrafts, for instance. We gathered examples of clothes, embroidery and jewelry from the Byzantine era, from the 19th century and from modern Greece."

To assemble the necessary material, the designers went to Greece, toured museums and ruins and, with the aid of the Greek government, composed lists of suitable items. They found Greek museums that make plaster reproductions of ancient Greek statues for exhibit in museums throughout the world. Surprisingly exact in texture, sheen and form, these reproductions are made by pouring plaster into a plaster mold, then finishing the piece with paint and polish until, says Marquart, "it is impossible for most people to tell the original from the repoduction." He ordered several for exhibit in Montreal.

Marquart and his colleagues had only three months from the time they took on the project until the exhibit opened. In that time, statues had to be reproduced in Greece and shipped by boat to Montreal, artifacts gathered, and photographs made of Greek vase paintings (which were often of Olympic performers) in museums throughout Europe. And because the Greek government gave final approval of all artifacts, it was not certain until the last minute just what would arrive.

The designers solved this problem by making mockups of the exhibit devices and positioning them, solving traffic flow and placement problems ahead of time so that artifacts could simply be placed in the finished display at the last minute.

In the exhibit's Olympic section, photos of vase paintings were juxtaposed with life-size statues and with ancient Olympic sports artifacts. For instance, an ancient discus was shown with its modern counterpart. In addition, visitors were channeled into three audio-visual displays. One dealt with trade and industry in modern Greece, a second with Greek vase photos, showing the paintings of performing athletes, and the third was a slide-show tour of ancient Olympia, featuring slides of present ruins, models and renderings.

Client: Greek Government
Design firm: Jacques Guillon/ Designers, Inc., Montreal
Designers: Jacques S. Guillon, Morley I. Smith, Consulting Partners: Laurent Marquart, Partner-in-Charge: Luc Courchesnes and Guy Demers
Architect: Dimitri, Dimakopoulos & Associates
Consultant: Binette & Associates (audio-visual)
Fabricator: Disney Display

4. Artifacts and graphics illustrate various events of ancient Olympics.
5. End of Olympic area; beginning of Greek mythology section.
6. Artifacts of Greek "traditional" period.
7. Detail of navigation industry showcase.
8. Plastic industry cases.

47/Exhibition Design

Fire!

In 1933, fire destroyed 220,000 acres of Oregon's Tillamook Forest. That's 343.75 square miles, an area as large as that of New York City and Boston combined. The fire was the largest single forest burn in U.S. history. But in 1976, the most recent year for which figures are available, 241,699 forest fires raged across the country, consuming 5,129,926 acres of woodland. Only 7 per cent of these fires were started by lightning. Man started the rest.

"Fire!", an exhibit at Portland, Oregon's Western Forestry Center, uses the Tillamook fire as an example of how fires are caused, what happens during a fire, and how the forest recovers. Though there is general public awareness, experts feel, about the need to prevent fires, people are still uncertain about how forest fires start. Though it may be a well-known fact, for instance, that if you toss a lighted cigarette into a pile of dry leaves you will start a fire, it is not so widely known that an automobile or motorcycle exhaust is hotter than a lighted cigarette and will ignite a pile of pine needles or a swatch of dry grass on contact. A hot chain-saw exhaust can do the same thing.

A visitor enters the Forestry Center's exhibit area and descends a ramp past graphic panels documenting some of the largest and more notorious forest fires. Designers of the David Strong Design Group used reds and oranges on these panels, which they placed among the charred remains of tree trunks. Farther along in this rampside area is introductory information about the Tillamook fire, leading to the exhibit's central focus, an audio-visual presentation of the Tillamook burn.

The board of the Western Forestry Center, a non-profit institution, came to Strong wanting a diorama. Strong took the idea and expanded it into a 15-minute slide show, projected onto two large, curving screens, 8' high and 15' long. On the floor beneath the front screen is a topographic model of the Tillamook Forest, and on it projectors cast light outlining the fire's spread, from its tiny beginning to its consummation of 344 square miles. The spread over the model is dramatic enough, but the audience watches this spread while screens in front and in back of them show slides taken in the midst of a forest fire's fury and a soundtrack plays the roars and cracks of a mammoth burn.

The story of the Tillamook fire is one of community involvement. Through a bond issue, residents in the area made replanting possible. Local groups (boy scouts, schools, churches, etc.) followed professionals into the forest, planting seedlings. Now, 45 years later, though the forest has had two major burns since 1933, the area is ready for harvesting.

Throughout the exhibit the David Strong Design Group uses natural finished woods and orange, red and rust colors. An area beyond the audio-visual display shows how forest fires start and how forestry departments study weather patterns to predict times at which fires are most likely. Using a series of photomurals, panels of text and artifacts, the exhibit then explains how fires are suppressed. On display are radios, helmets, smoke masks, hoses, axes, shovels, satellite maps, photo-reconnaissance infrared photos, and a live teletype printing out weather conditions and fire warnings in the northwest. Displayed next to today's fire-fighting tools are those used in 1933, some merely fastened to the wall, some behind plexiglass on pedestals.

At the end of the exhibit is a push-button area that lets a viewer become a fire boss during a burn. On a screen appear slides of a forest fire. An illuminated panel states the situation and asks the viewer to push a button nearest the solution he thinks correct. Envision, for instance, a fire-fighting crew isolated while cutting a break through the forest ahead of a fire. If the fire, pushed by wind, jumps over them and surrounds them, what should you, the fire boss, do?

Client: Western Forestry Center (Portland, OR)
Design firm: David Strong Design Group, Seattle, WA
Designers: David Strong, Gary LaComa, Vince Balisky, Joe Maricich
Consultants: Spectrum Studios; Thomas McCarthy (writer); Jim Fisher (forester)
Fabricator: All West Display

1.

Exhibition Design/48

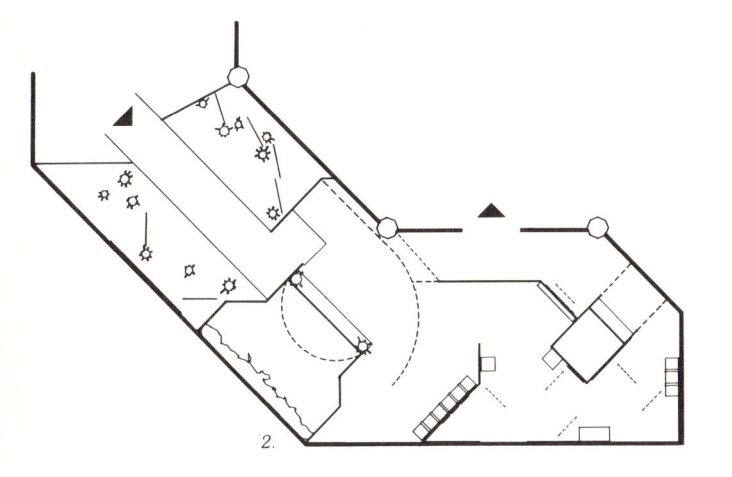

1. Tillamook Forest model.
2. Plan.
3. Fire simulator lets visitors make fire-fighting decisions.
4. Charred tree trunks stand in front of panels commemorating famous forest fires.

5.

6.

7.

8.

5. Photos and artifacts illustrate advantages of decision to restore Tillamook after fire.
6. Fire-fighting tools and devices.
7, 8. How a fire team's communication center works.

Satellites Hall

Rockets and space satellites, seen up close, lose much of their romance. What's glamorous about a collection of wires, diodes, batteries and antennas? Part of the problem confronting John Schmid Associates in designing the Satellites Hall for the National Air and Space Museum in Washington, D.C., was to capture the romance along with the robotry. Another large part of the problem was to fit a welter of rockets (ranging in size from 3' to 60' high) and satellites into a 7000-sq. ft. space beneath a 20' ceiling with enough information accompanying each item to explain what it is and what it does.

Schmid and his staff solved the latter problem by hanging name panels (Formica-covered gator board) next to each ceiling-hung satellite and running text on color-coded sections of free-standing, perimeter, plywood floor panels. Casebook jurors were impressed with the amount of information presented. It was easy to read, they felt, and easy to follow. Schmid achieved this by giving the masses of technical information on the back-lighted panels a crisp, highly articulated look, orderly and precise, using a Times Bold typeface.

The romance came out just as well. Perhaps romance is in the eye of the beholder, but Schmid helps the eye by bombarding the ear with satellite and rocket sounds. The museum had suggested an ambient dark color. Schmid made this color black, the color of space, on walls and ceiling, against which the polished aluminum satellites glint and sparkle. Lighting interferes minimally with this contrast because the perimeter panels, beneath the hanging displays, are back-lighted. Schmid's lighting adds much to the exhibit, twinkling off the ceiling-hung satellites and, at night, washing the rockets positioned in the huge gallery windows, beckoning to passersby.

To put one in the right frame of mind for satellite viewing, Schmid designed an exhibit entrance, a transition between the rest of the museum building and the Satellite Hall. This break is simply a ramp leading up from the main museum corridor through a tunnel, lined with a photo transparency of earth seen from an orbiting satellite. Visitors emerge from the tunnel into the satellite-hung gallery with its 20' ceiling.

Three of the exhibit's rockets—those taller than 20'—had to go in wells just behind the gallery's 115'-long window wall.

In preliminary meetings the Air and Space Museum gave Schmid a list of the exhibit's 12 rockets and 40 satellites and told him they would suspend the satellites from the center of the ceiling. This placement left Schmid the task of presenting the satellites, which averaged about 4' in diameter with their antennae extended, on a human scale. He did this by keeping the height of the free-standing, continuous-information panels on the gallery floor at close to human height—no higher than 8' to 10'—and placing them near the building's interior wall. "The design approach to the hall was to think of it as a single environment," says Schmid, "rather than as a series of individual, highly structured units."

Out of a $180,000 budget for installation and fabrication, Schmid had to provide a ladder and viewing platform, from which visitors can peer into the innards of a cut-away Viking rocket, and provide steel structural supports for all rockets over 15' tall (with two exceptions: the Agena and the 60' Viking were installed and supported by the museum).

Because of the budget, a planned film explaining how a satellite stays in orbit became a slide show, but everything else fit the space, the budget and the five-month design-installation schedule. Presented in an octagonal theater, between the rocketry and satellite sections of the show, slides offer an introduction to satellites and space exploration. Visitors stand looking at the theater walls lighted by ceiling spots. Through an outer glass layer they see a mural of a medieval scholar gazing out at space; then, as the lights dim slowly, they stand surrounded by a star field, produced by back-lighting shining through random holes etched in a mirror behind the mural scrim. Against this star field slides appear on three screens.

Client: National Air and Space Museum, Smithsonian Institution (Washington, D.C.)
Design firm: John Schmid Associates, Reston, VA
Designers: John Schmid, Don Reithlingshoefer, Bill Simon, Judy Johnston, Peter Barna, Carl Schiller
Fabricator: DCA Exhibits

1. Section showing rocketry for launching satellites.
2. Weather satellites.

Exhibition Design/52

Weather Satellites

Observing the World's Weather   SMS

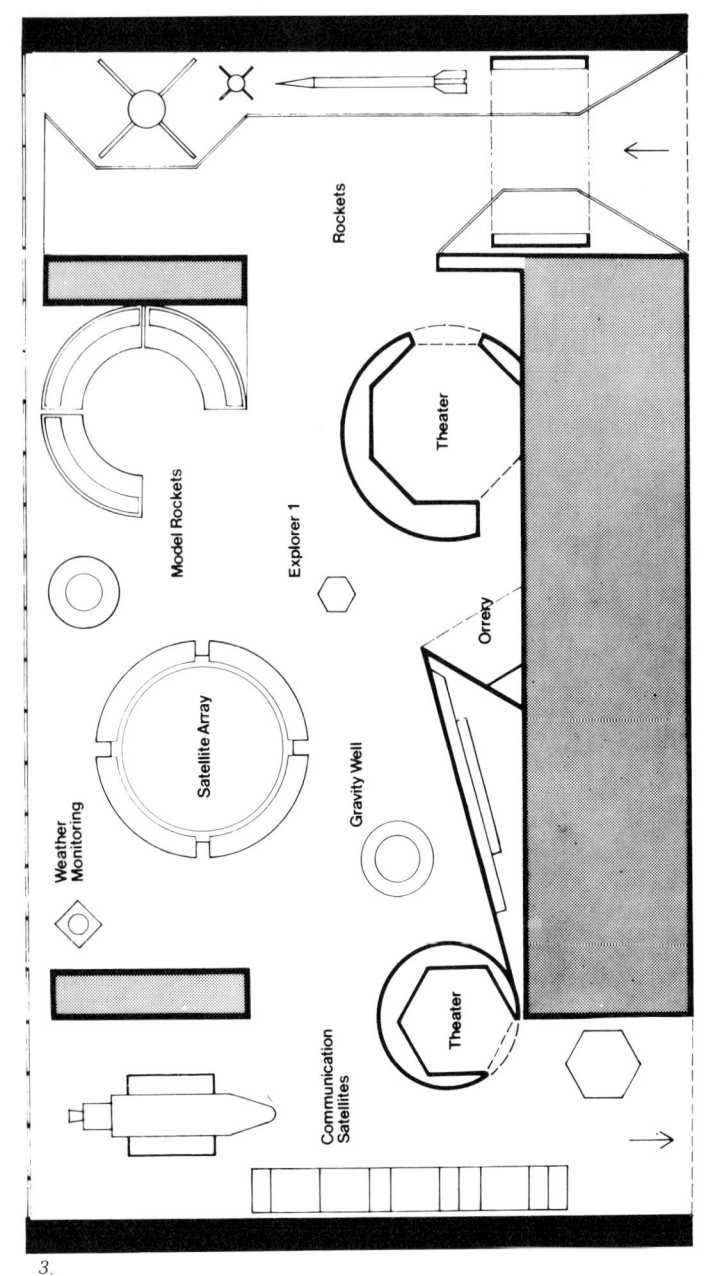

3. Foor plan.
4. A ceiling full of satellites.

Exhibition Design/54

Satellites

Spacecraft Systems

Montreal Museum of Fine Arts

"You see it rarely," said one of the Casebook jurors, referring to the display cases designed by Jacques Guillon/Designers for the Montreal Museum of Fine Arts. What the juror meant, of course, was that most exhibits in museums and elsewhere use standard, manufactured display cases. But the Guillon designers wanted a case that would complement the architecture of the museum's new extension. The glass, oak, and concrete cases do blend nicely with the extension's glass and concrete walls and polished wood floors.

Resting on two concrete bases each weighing 175 pounds, the cases are unquestionably stable. "We purposely decided to favor strength and stability rather than ease of movement," says Guillon partner Laurent Marquart. Strength was needed for security, they felt—not just security from theft but from accident also, such as someone bumping into a case. And since the Montreal museum is near a heavy-traffic artery with trucks and heavy equipment rumbling by most of the day, they wanted to be sure that delicate porcelain objects wouldn't vibrate to the edge of the case's interior shelves, fall off and break. To prevent this vibration, not only are the cases seated securely on their concrete bases, but also their shelves, supported by chrome and stainless-steel rods and held by vinyl extrusions, are designed to vibrate to a different frequency from the cases.

Despite their weight, the cases are relatively easy to

1. Outside graphics signal opening of renovated museum.
2, 3. Glass, oak and concrete artifact cases.

Exhibition Design/56

3.

57/Exhibition Design

move. Morley Smith went to the trouble of designing a rubber-tired steel hand-cart to fit the pockmarked concrete bases. Since each base rests on nylon discs, one of which is adjustable to insure that each base is precisely level, the cart can slip beneath the base, lift it, wheel it to a different spot, lower it into place and slide out. Bases (two for most cases) are positioned exactly so that an oak platform will fit into the deep, crossed grooves in each cruciform base.

This oak platform, besides serving as a surface for artifacts, holds lighting and has a small drawer into which silica gell can be slipped if the cases' contents need low humidity. Into grooves in this platform fit the cases' glass sides, each about 8mm thick. "There are no metal edges, no hard edges," says Morley Smith. Rather, there are gaps between glass panels, filled by a clear, flexible, vinyl extrusion. To hold the glass sides together, Smith designed a chrome corner piece which screws through adjacent glass panels. It takes a two-pronged tool, specially designed for the fastening unit, to unscrew it, and this feature aids security. On top fits another piece of glass or a lighting box, with a grid to hide its fluorescent tubes. Wiring runs through a chrome rod, placed at one corner of the case, through the base to floor plugs, positioned throughout the museum.

"Elegant" is what the Casebook jurors called these cases, praising especially their detailing. "It is the kind of thing you wish you had done," said one.

How do curators place

4, 5. Pictogram system guides visitors to galleries within museum. The one shown here is for Amerindian Art.
6. Specially designed hand-truck moves concrete bases.
7. Typical sign elements.
8. Wall labels.
9. Room full of cases.

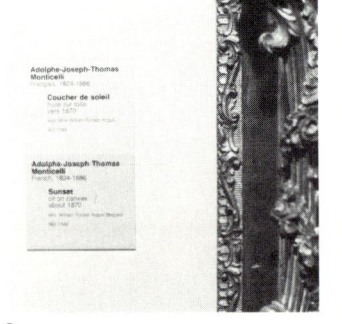

Exhibition Design/58

9.

59/Exhibition Design

objects in the cases? Smith made it unnecessary to disassemble the entire unit each time something has to be repositioned. The longer side panels are on a sliding track, and by using a Smith-designed tripod to support the glass once it is slid more than half way out, curators can open the case and work inside it.

As another facet of their museum assignment, Guillon/Designers created signing for the museum, inside and out. Inside, they devised a pictogram system to guide visitors to particular galleries. "We rejected abstract or stylized symbols," says Laurent Marquart, who headed the graphic design team. "Abstract symbols would impose a barrier between the museum and the visitor; they would need a translator." Marquart's solution was to select a typical work of art from a specific collection (e.g., a stone relief for the Egyptian collection; a porcelain vase for the Chinese collection). He placed a black-and-white photo copy of the work on a plaque, color-coded according to the century the collection represents and its geographical origin. These pictograms serve as a tease, pulling people into exhibits the way an appetizer excites enjoyment of a meal. But the designers wish, in retrospect, that they had used brighter colors or colors with greater contrasts.

Guillon/Designers also prepared maps and a museum guide leaflet. Elsewhere in the new extension, they did the interior design for a sales shop, a rental gallery and a lounge.

10. Pictogram for Africa/Oceania gallery.
11. Concrete bases rest on nylon discs.

Client: The Montreal Museum of Fine Arts
Design firm: Jacques Guillon/Designers, Inc., Montreal
Designers: Jacques S. Guillon, Morley L. Smith, Pierre Tardif, Tim Skeene, Laurent Marquart, Luc Courchesnes, Roger Labastrou, Denis Gauthier
Consultants: Arcop Architects; Latham Stolow
Fabricators: Metal Works (exhibit system); Trans Canada Display (graphics)

Exhibition Design/60

Celebrate '76

The banners, bins, bread loaves, beams and boxes hanging from an aluminum framework in New York's Rockefeller Center during the summer of '76 were part of a Bicentennial exhibit. The exhibit focused on the contributions of immigrants to New York City and the U.S., reminding everyone who looked that most Americans either come from somewhere else or have forebears who did. Who are we? Where did we come from? What did we bring with us? What have we accomplished? These were the exhibit's themes; and such was the respect with which it was received that it remained untouched by graffiti artists or other vandals, though it stood outside for three Manhattan summer months.

"The people at Rockefeller Center were greatly concerned about vandalism," says William Kissiloff, who designed "Celebrate '76." "But nothing happened."

Set up atop the flower garden that forms a central channel in the broad walkway connecting Fifth Avenue with Rockefeller Center's outdoor skating rink-restaurant, the exhibit led off with a photographic blowup, 10' wide and 2½' high, laminated in fiberglass, of an immigrant family sighting the Statue of Liberty and New York harbor from shipboard. Above this, stretched from an aluminum pipe framework, were colored nylon banners, 2' by 12', with a representation of the Statue of Liberty sewn into them. Kissiloff hung everything from this aluminum framework, a Nu-rail system containing 2000' of piping bolted

1. Plan.
2. Aerial photo of exhibit.

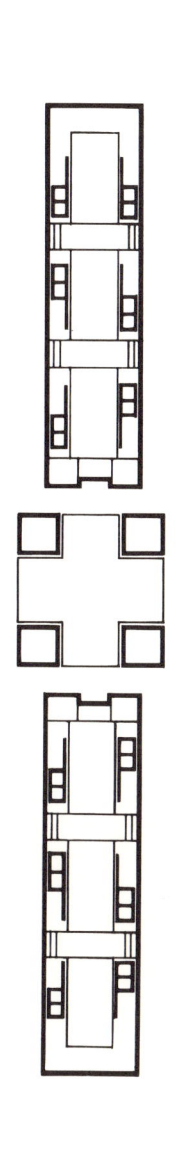

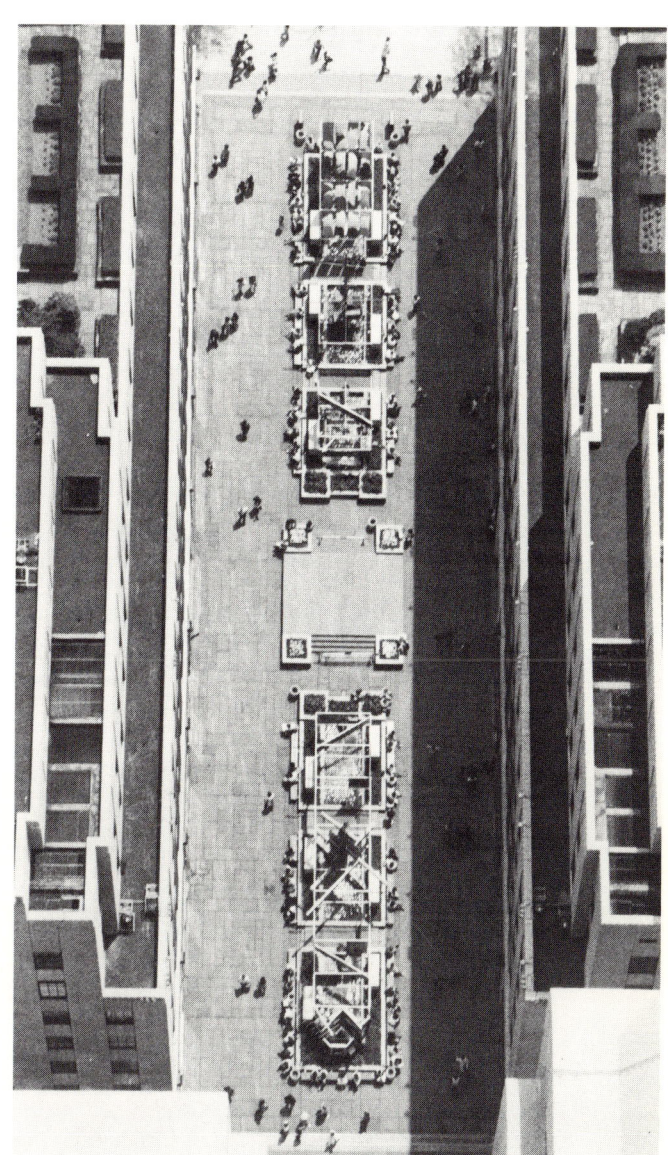

1.

2.

61/Exhibition Design

3. Exhibit was mounted on 2000' of steel piping.
4. Graphic panels and artifact cases were bolted to piping system.
5. Statue of Liberty banners mark exhibit starting point.

together with more than 200 connectors. He anchored it in concrete footings poured in the flower beds and hidden discreetly by new ivy. At the top, wires stretched to flanking buildings secured the system against fluky summer winds whipping through the Manhattan canyons.

Larger graphics of people, or buildings, were screened onto 2' by 10' panels of Kydex and riveted to the aluminum frame. Twenty-four lighted display boxes (3' by 3'), constructed of Kydex with Lexan windows, held religious artifacts, passenger lists, passports, coffee beans, tea, and the different breads of ethnic groups. Kissiloff also had New York street signs with ethnic names (Edenwald Avenue, Columbus Place, Ericsson Street) bolted to the aluminum framework. There were pieces of sports equipment and building girders (constructed of wood to reduce their weight to 450 pounds from the two tons they would have weighed in steel), a 30' wooden mast, plastic sausages, and more banners with images of an eagle, a star and buildings of the Manhattan skyline sewn onto them. Most graphics were in black-and-white or sepia. Everything held up under summer heat and rain, despite some fading.

As a typeface for blocks of explanatory text and one-line captions, Kissiloff used Souvenir, which he felt had the "quality and warmth to go with the history and nostalgia" of the exhibit, and also "to get away from Helvetica."

In the exhibit's center, midway between Fifth Avenue

Exhibition Design/62

Celebrate 76
New York City is a mix of countless
nationalities—a living mosaic of people,
customs, and cultures.
This exhibit highlights our common
immigrant heritage and salutes the
contributions made by the City's
diverse peoples.

and the skating rink-restaurant, Kissiloff put a raised dance floor, which the client, Rockefeller Center, kept vibrating with ethnic dance groups, musicians and bands.

Client: Rockefeller Center, Inc. (New York)
Design firm: Kissiloff Associates, Inc., New York
Designer: William Kissiloff
Fabricator: Exhibitgroup New York

6.

6. Fire Department artifacts.
7. Rockefeller Center's RCA building towers over exhibit photos of City Hall and Central Park.
8-11. Exhibit fragments. Steel girders in Fig. 11 were made of wood.

7.

65/Exhibition Design

Food for Life

In the first eight months of its existence, "Food for Life," the nutritional exhibit at Chicago's Museum of Science and Industry, drew more visitors than either the White Sox or the Cubs—Chicago's major-league baseball teams—did that summer. But what pleased the exhibit's sponsor, Swift & Company, a division of Esmark, Inc., even more was that each visitor to their exhibit spent an average of 20 minutes taking it in.

Time span was what Esmark/Swift executives were preoccupied with when they first outlined their needs to The Burdick Group in San Francisco. They wanted a replacement for their original "Food for Life" exhibit, which had run at the Museum of Science and Industry for 22 years but was holding people's attention for an average of only three minutes.

Bruce Burdick, who prides himself on the fresh look his firm gives each project it tackles, went into the Esmark/Swift problem with a thoroughness that led him through a four-month computer course and eventually took him to Japan.

The new exhibit radically shifts both what the public sees and how it sees it. Original emphasis in "Food for Life" was on livestock and feed production. Now, it is on human food and nutrition. "We wanted to create an abstract market place," explains Burdick. "We wanted the food actually to be there, because nutritional decisions are made in the market. In this setting Burdick hoped to demonstrate the results of food shopping decisions—to show people the nutritional values of items they pile in their shopping carts. Further, to drive these values home, he wanted somehow to make the exhibit personal, to acquaint all visitors with their own nutritional needs and show how various foods fill them. The final exhibit does all this so successfully that the technique, though expensive, may see increasing exhibit use.

What Burdick did, working with an overall exhibit budget of $1,000,000, was to offer visitors the chance to feed their physical dimensions into a computer. On demand, the computer gives back personal nutritional information based on individual physical profiles.

At the exhibit entrance visitors, using a pocket calculator-type key arrangement (designed by The Burdick Group), give the computer their age, height, weight, and sex. Then, at terminals in 11 locations throughout the exhibit, they can ask the computer up to 50 questions about foods and get personal responses on monitor screens. For instance, one terminal is set up next to a 12'-high rectangular glass case holding trays of food. The case rotates, bringing everything into view so that the visitor can select a meal. He tells the computer what he's chosen to eat, punching the information on the calculator-type keyboard, and the computer tells him such things as whether or not he's short on protein or calories.

There is no question that everyone likes the computer's personal approach. But its popularity may be a weakness. Long lines often develop at each terminal, and many persons wander off rather than wait. Esmark is in the process of alleviating this problem by adding more terminals. At the same time, a phone hook-up is being installed linking boards and screens in school classrooms across the country to the museum-located computer.

Bruce Burdick sees the computer as the most satisfying element of his design for Esmark..."to run the risk of whether it would really work, and to see that it did by the smiles on people's faces as they use the exhibit."

Still, there is much more than that to the 7700-square-foot exhibit. For if the computer is an innovative exhibit idea, the Casebook jury found the wealth of

1.

1. Food served elegantly is compared with fast-food service. Nutritional value is usually the same.
2. Computer terminal in market setting gives individual information about food selected by visitor.

Exhibition Design/66

If you have made an error
PUSH ERASE

If you would like to start over
PUSH RESET

accompanying details equally impressive. "Rich" is what one juror called it, and indeed there is enough going on, enough to look at and do, to keep even the most restless at bay temporarily. Burdick packed the entire exhibit, not just the market area, with 13,000 individual items of "food" made of wax and vinyl in Japan. Though the Japanese turn out rivers of these decoy foods for display in restaurants and markets, their manufacturers seemed baffled, Burdick reports, by Twinkies and by the larger sizes of American bread loaves and vegetables such as artichokes.

In all, the exhibit has 19 distinct areas.

In one, a table is set with food as prepared by a French restaurant, by a fast-food chain such as McDonald's, and as sold in vending machines. Sound accompanies the display—the sounds of glassware and knives and forks in the French restaurant, the calls of the McDonald's clerks, and the clicks of vending machines. The message is that, however different in approach, price and service, the various outlets offer essentially the same food with the same nutritive value.

In another area is a bicycle hooked to an overhead dial. When you pump on the bicycle, the dial tells you how many calories you would burn if you kept up that effort for a given period of time. From your seat on the bike you can see a greenhouse where vegetables are growing.

Cooks in a test kitchen elsewhere in the exhibit prepare different recipes and food blends, and occasionally an exhibit viewer is asked to sample Swift products. A food technology case displays items tracing the history of human food and ways of storing it — from stuffing it into sections of intestine and cooking it, to contemporary soft-food packs.

A chick hatcher, carried over from the old exhibit, has an incubator, eggs and lots of hatching yellow chicks.

The Burdick Group designed the glass cases holding the food displays throughout the exhibit. Though steel frames surround glass sections of each case, the overlapping individual glass panels are actually held in place by steel bumper logs.

The typeface, Century Schoolbook, goes splendidly with the bins and baskets of a traditional market.

"The history of man is linked to the evolution of his food," says Burdick. "No one could paint the Sistine Chapel ceiling while busy hunting or gathering food."

Client: Esmark/Swift & Co. (Chicago)
Design firm: The Burdick Group, San Francisco
Designers: Bruce Burdick, Stephen Hamilton, Andrew Kramer
Fabricator: General Exhibits and Displays, Inc.

3. Visitors punch computer keyboard beneath onions made in Japan.
4. When visitors pump bicycle pedals, dial tells them how many calories per hour they are burning.
5. Fermentation explained.

Exhibition Design/68

FERTILIZATION EXPANDS FARMING

Because grains, peas, and beans grow abundantly with minimum care, they became early basic crops. In time, man discovered that they grew even better in soil enriched by decaying plant life. He began to 'fertilize' by spreading decomposing plants—including his excess peas and beans—on his farm land. He also learned that bigger and better crops were produced in soil containing other kinds of organic matter: human and animal excrement, wood ashes, and buried fish proved to be particularly effective.

BETTER FOOD FROM FERMENTATION

As man learned to control his food supply, civilization developed and probably reached its first peak in Sumeria, part of Mesopotamia's Fertile Crescent, around 3000 B.C. Sumerians introduced grapes, figs, peaches, melons, and other fruits. They discovered fermentation—and produced the first wine and beer. Leavened bread, caused by fermentation in wheat dough, came later in ancient Egypt. By leavening their bread, the Egyptians made it tastier and more edible. A new dimension was added to food processing.

Maps: Their Art and Their Science

Maps have something to say to everyone; they are as useful to a dreamer as to a mariner. A map will help you plan the future, remember the past, save your life. Viewed historically, maps offer guides to man's understanding of his world. All of this was immediately apparent to visitors to "Maps: Their Art and Their Science," a temporary exhibit at the American Museum of Natural History in mid-1977.

Fortunately for the exhibit's designers, Donovan and Green, maps are also colorful and wonderfully decorative. The design problem became one of logical organization within a system of display that would not overpower the maps while guiding visitors past them.

With the maps were globes and tools used in mapmaking, such as a laser surveying device with a digital readout.

Donovan and Green started by breaking the show into five parts:

1. New York City—antique and contemporary maps of the city.
2. History of Mapmaking—development of maps documented with antique atlases and maps.
3. How Maps Are Made—from the earliest hand-drawn maps through printing techniques to aerial, computer-made maps.
4. How Maps Are Used—how museums, scientists, geologists, planners, architects, astronauts, etc., use today's maps.
5. Maps of the Mind—maps made by poets, writers and artists, mythological

1.

2.

Exhibition Design/70

fantasy maps.

In all, Donovan and Green collected more than 300 items and hung them against backgrounds of natural muslin, which provided what they describe as a "warm background for both boldly and subtly colored objects." The Casebook jurors spoke of the color's "restraint" and noted that the settings didn't destroy the delicate beauty of the maps.

The muslin backing was placed on wall panels or in cases based on 42" modules. Cases were 18" deep, 11' high and 42" wide. Wall panels were 42" square, while occasional free-standing panels measured 11' tall by 42" wide. Both panels and cases were faced with plexiglass on which descriptive texts were screened. Free-standing panels and cases were then stacked and juxtaposed to form viewing areas, barriers and alleys, guiding visitors logically through the exhibit.

Donovan and Green had two and a half months from the time they took on the assignment until the opening, and their greatest problem was a familiar one: assembling priceless objects in time to position them and prepare descriptive material. Museums, libraries, historical societies and private donors were willing to loan maps from their collections but didn't want them sitting around unmounted and unguarded. Many items were shipped to the American Museum at the last moment. "Delivery was postponed until the cases were up and ready to hold the artifacts," recalls Michael Donovan.

3.

1. Globes were part of map exhibit.
2, 3. Cases and free-standing panels were juxtaposed to form viewing areas.
4. Map-making tools were also part of exhibit.

4.

71/Exhibition Design

For a typeface, the designers chose Century Schoolbook because they felt a serif face was appropriate for maps and because it is highly legible.

Some of the more memorable maps:

• Map of Tokeido Road, Japan, 1640; a folded map 20′ long and 10″ high, one of a series of five that showed in delicate ink and washes every detail of the road between Tokyo and Kyoto.

• Carved wooden map, New Guinea, 18th century; a carved stick 2′ long and 3″ wide indicating water holes.

• Chinese scroll map, 17th century, 30′ long, of the coastline of China.

• U.S. geologic survey map, 1977, 8′ high by 40′ long; an infrared photo-mosaic map of the U.S.

• Anderson isometric map, 1977; midtown Manhattan, indicating in isometric drawing every detail of each building and street.

5.

5, 6. Map tables.
7. Floor plan.

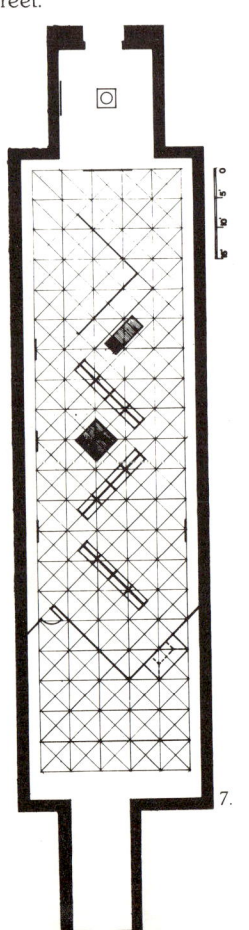

6.

7.

Client: American Museum of Natural History (New York)
Design firm: Donovan and Green, Inc., New York
Designers: Michael Donovan, Nancy Green, Arthur Natale
Consultants: Margaret Cooper (writer), Sidney Harenstein (curator)
Fabricator: C.D. Industries, Inc.

Three IBM Exhibits

During 1977, Carlos Ramirez & Albert H. Woods, Inc., designed the three IBM exhibits shown here. All three have a similarity of appearance, a family look, just as IBM computers and tabulators do, and so are presented together. Part of their similarity lies in the inevitable similarity any exhibits displaying a lot of IBM equipment and innards would have. Another part stems from inclusion, in two of the exhibits, of a flexible light-box-display platform designed by Carlos Ramirez from polished oak, acrylic and steel. And, too, pervading all three installations is the crisp, precise elegance both IBM and Carlos Ramirez & Albert H. Woods, Inc., desire in design.

1. Flexible Exhibition System

IBM likes to move its exhibits around, exposing them to people everywhere, demystifying the computer and personalizing the corporation. IBM is trying to increase its museum exposure and, in addition, is thinking seriously of setting up temporary exhibits on college campuses.

The exhibit shown here is in Baltimore's new Maryland Science Center. It's the first installation of a flexible exhibition system, which will make this IBM exhibit and others like it adaptable to different spaces and fairly easy to pack and ship.

The basis of the flexible system is an English oak case, 2' by 4' by 11'. Placed on the floor, the case becomes a platform that will hold pieces of IBM equipment, a standard calculator, for instance, which may weigh 800 pounds or

1. Floor plan for "Evolution of the Computer."
2. Entrance to exhibit set up in Maryland Science Center.

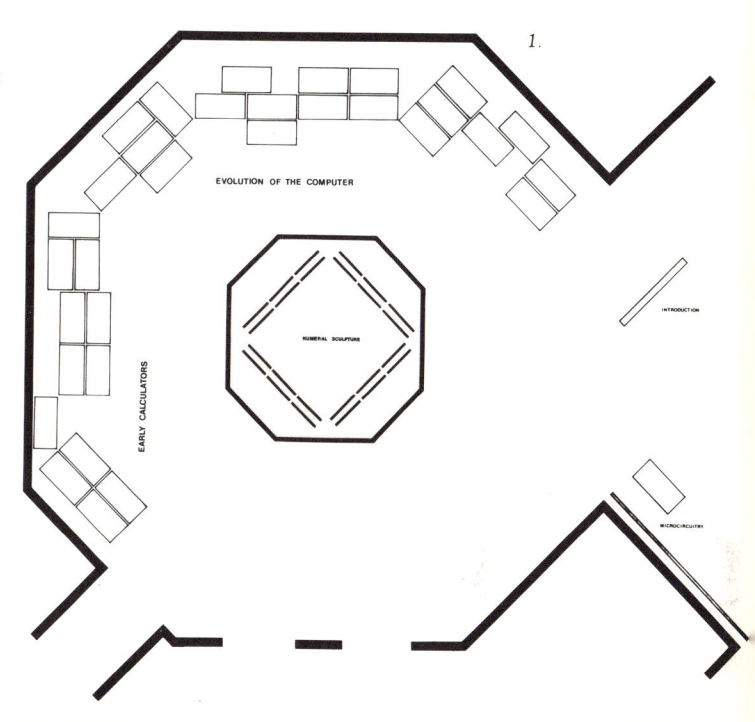

more. Moreover, these cases, topped with acrylic, become light boxes, and when stacked two or three deep, raise the viewing surface to near-waist height. Panels slide in and out of grooves in the 1½"-thick oak walls at three different levels (top, bottom, middle), giving the boxes a remarkable variety of roles. For instance, by slipping an acrylic panel into the top, a flat board lined with fluorescent tubes into the bottom, and a translucent surface with transparencies and graphics into the center, you turn the case into a light box. By stacking several units and sliding panels in only at the very bottom and very top, you can give the boxes increasing depth. And if you slip in an individual steel panel with a Kapex surface (Kapex is a cork-plastic mixture used in bulletin boards), the case becomes a pedestal for heavy IBM equipment. Kapex has the ability to regain its original shape once the gouging legs of heavy equipment are removed.

Grooves in the cases' corners are raceways for wiring and air ducts for ventilation. It was the need to keep tangles of wires off the floor while channeling them in and out of the cases that led designers Ramirez & Woods to develop stainless-steel posts. These posts fit through perforations in the Kapex-surfaced top panels. Seen in cross section, the posts are square and hollow so that wiring can run through them to light, say, a panel of text atop the post. These posts become supports for railings or for large vertical billboard-like panels and their cantilevered canister lights.

For transport, the cases and the exhibit that goes with them slip into a modification of standard shipping cases.

Maryland Science Center's installation shows how early calculating machines evolved into today's computers. Ramirez & Woods arranged the exhibit around a sculpture of laminated plywood numerals.

Client: IBM Corp. (Armonk, NY)
Design firm: Carlos Ramirez & Albert H. Woods, Inc., New York
Designer: Carlos Ramirez
Fabricator: DeLuca deCaprá

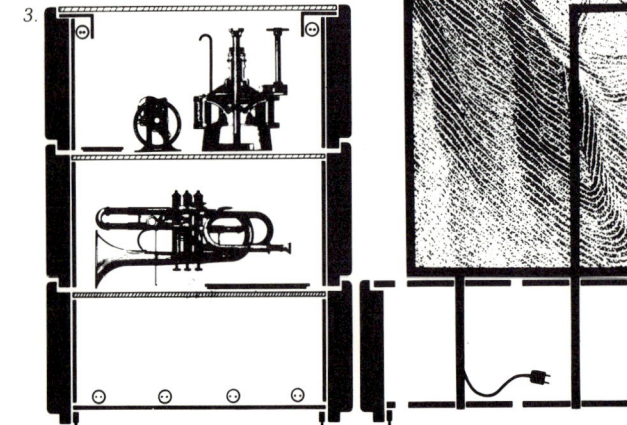

Exhibition Design/74

3. Cutaway reverse-negative of exhibit detail.
4, 5. Exhibit system consists of stackable oak cases. Topped with Kapex-surfaced steel panels punctured with holes, boxes become platforms for heavy items or standards for graphic panels on steel legs.
6, 7. In center of room is sculpture of plywood numbers.

75/Exhibition Design

2. Permanent Exhibition on the History of Computing

What was once a window exhibit in IBM's New York City showroom is now installed in the California Museum of Science and Industry in Los Angeles.

Designer Carlos Ramirez of Carlos Ramirez & Albert H. Woods, Inc., treated the move as a chance to spread out and, through the use of individual lighting, dramatize. "To build another storefront exhibit within the museum would have been a simple solution," says Ramirez, but he welcomed especially the opportunity to do something about the glare and feeling of inaccessibility produced by the Madison Avenue showroom windows. Still, removing the windows opened the lid of security.

Conceived to show the computer's evolution from early mechanical calculating machines, through RAMAC, the vacuum-tubed computers of the '50s, to today's micro-circuited machines, the exhibit contains a lot of computer components—diodes, tubes, transistors, tape decks—most of them valuable. Ramirez's solution was to design waist-high showcases, running as barriers around the exhibit walls. These cases hold smaller items and graphics—models, components, transparencies. Photos and silk-screened graphics are positioned on the cases' cutaway Naugahyde surfaces and backlighted. Behind this glass-counter-walnut-showcase Ramirez placed larger items, such as cutaways of large computer components, on pedestals. Graphics on aluminum panels are either fastened directly to the wall or suspended from the ceiling. Lighting spots only individual items, silhouetting some, making others seem to float in the dim interior. On larger components pin spots pick out highlights.

An island formed of the flexible exhibit cases seen on pages 73-75 sits in the room's center. Surrounded by a stainless steel railing are antique calculating devices and steel-framed panels of graphic description.

Throughout the room Ramirez uses earth tones, complemented by IBM cobalt blue.

Client: IBM Corp. (Armonk, NY)
Design firm: Carlos Ramirez & Albert H. Woods, Inc., New York
Designer: Carlos Ramirez
Consultant: DeLuca deCapra
Fabricator: Bob Shultz

1.

1. IBM exhibit in California Museum of Science and Industry. Island holds antique calculators.
2. Plan.

77/Exhibition Design

3. Hanging panels carry explanatory texts.
4. Linear glass-covered case holds smaller items.
5. Continuous case becomes barrier protecting larger equipment behind it.

Exhibition Design/78

3. Architecture and Artifacts

In Atlanta, IBM gives visitors guided tours of its General Services Division headquarters, a contemporary concrete and glass structure by architects Thompson, Ventulett, Stainback and Associates. It has been IBM's penchant in the past to enhance its office workers' environment by providing fine art along with fine architecture. This art is usually contemporary, paintings and sculpture mounted on public walls in lobbies and corridors, in conference rooms, offices and reception areas. In Atlanta the art budget went for exhibits. But the difference was not as abrupt as you might think. Designers Ramirez & Woods chose artifacts with textures, colors and shapes that fit precise positions in the building. And they paid attention to how these items were mounted. "We arranged them as sculpture," says Carlos Ramirez. "We didn't just string them along walls. At the same time we treated them as more significant than just décor." Now, tour guides lead visitors past displays which, if art, nonetheless convey very specific messages about IBM's origins and status.

Ramirez & Woods positioned triangular wooden islands (some with cut-wood mosaic tops) throughout the building. On these platforms they placed early punchcard tabulating machines, clocks, typewriters, Dayton scales and other artifacts made by companies eventually amalgamated into International Business Machines. For some historic items, Ramirez & Woods designed elegant pedestals of polished wood, marble and etched glass. Smaller items, components, models—things which might easily be pilfered—are placed in glass cases with accompanying graphics.

Carlos Ramirez, who headed the design project, enjoyed particularly the challenge of designing settings for antique objects within the contemporary confines of a "severe glass and raw concrete" building.

Client: IBM General Services Div. (Atlanta)
Design firm: Carlos Ramirez & Albert H. Woods, Inc., New York
Designer: Carlos Ramirez
Fabricator: DeLuca deCapra

1. Antique punch card tabulator on triangular wooden island is displayed like sculpture in IBM's General Services Division Headquarters.

2, 4. Polished wood, marble and glass pedestals hold Dayton scales and equipment made by other companies that eventually combined into IBM.
3. Plan.
5. Hollerith early tabulating machines.
6. Electric accounting machines.

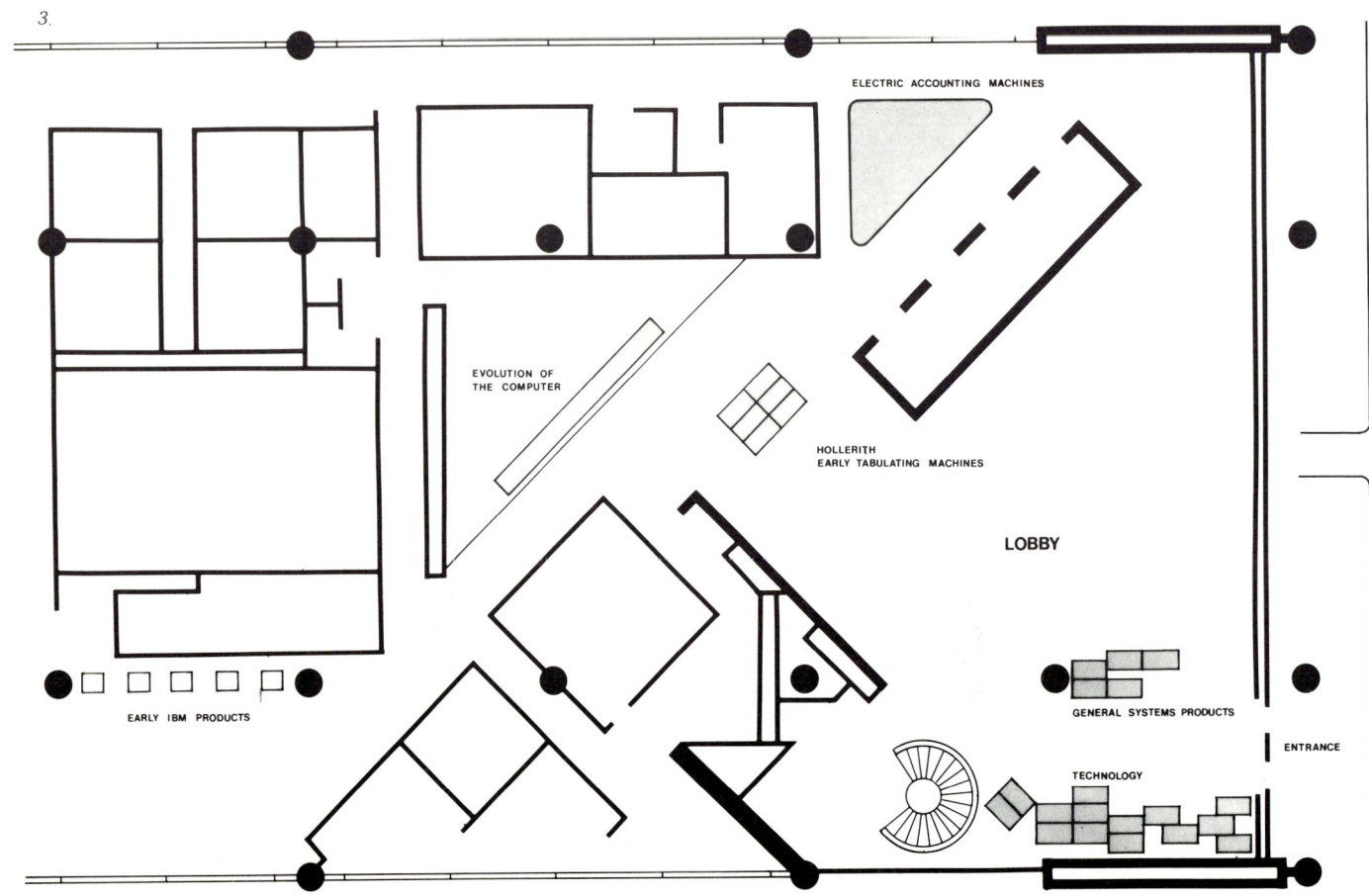

Exhibition Design/80

5.

81/Exhibition Design

Museum of Anthropology, University of British Columbia

The University of British Columbia created its Museum of Anthropology specifically to house the University's anthropological collection.

So successfully does the building, designed by Canadian architect Arthur C. Erickson, work together with the exhibits and the collections (mostly of northwest coast Canadian Indian artifacts), each supporting and intensifying the other, that to talk of them separately becomes impossible.

"The key to the whole project was that it was a small, specialized museum, going to be brand-new, starting from scratch," says Rudy Kovach, of Hopping, Kovach & Grinnel, who was in charge of the exhibit design.

In 1947, when Harry B. Hawthorn became the University's first professor of anthropology, and his wife, Audrey, became curator of the anthropological collections, they worked in cramped basement space beneath the University library. There, they assembled 16,000 to 20,000 artifacts, largely of coastal northwest Indian tribes, such as the Kwakuitl and Haida.

"For three decades we worked in one basement room of the library; there we arranged the exhibits, taught classes, had special events and stored the growing number of items in nooks and crannies which we were allowed to make into cupboards and safe-rooms," writes Audrey Hawthorn.

Then, with relative suddenness, in the spring of 1973 construction started on the new museum. Made possible by a $2.5-million grant from the Canadian federal government, supported by contributions from the National Museums of Canada and the University of British Columbia, the museum opened in mid-1976; and abruptly the curators, the collection, the entire department of anthropology had space, light and splendor.

Huge totem poles, some 60' high, carved from 3' diameter trees, were taken from storage in a shed and placed in the museum's Great Hall and just outside it, around what will become a lake. Architect Erickson sited the museum on a cliff looking out to sea; and seen from some angles, the totem poles seem to be standing at the edge of a tidal inlet, as they originally did in Indian villages.

Inside, the building is low-key and rhythmic (Erickson speaks of the cadence of his work), letting the art unfold as you pass through. One enters through massive doors, carved especially for the museum by contemporary Indian artists, beneath a descending series of concrete posts and beams. Drawn by light far ahead, one moves down a ramp past examples of northwest coastal Indian carving, arranged by tribe, and displayed on concrete projections rising out of the ramp. As the ramp descends gradually, the ceiling begins to rise (beneath an ascending series of posts and beams) and the walls to spread until one is in the Great Hall, flooded by light entering through gigantic windows, surrounded by totem poles looking off into space.

Adjacent to the Great Hall in a lower-ceilinged section is a collection of miniature carvings, housed in floor-to-ceiling glass cases. These cases have slits rising between sections of tempered glass so that air from the museum, controlled in temperature and humidity, can enter and circulate.

Behind this gallery of miniatures is a small theater, designed by Rudy Kovach for ritual ceremonies and dances. And behind the theater is the museum's largest area—its open storage.

This innovative combination of display and storage houses, in 10,000 sq. ft. (compared to 25,000 sq. ft. in the museum's main exhibit areas), the bulk of the museum's artifacts. Kovach and his designers designed free-standing stacks of Perspex-topped drawers, which form islands throughout the space. Glass-covered shelves line the walls. For large items the designers fashioned walk-in glass cases. Everything is on view to both research scholar and casual visitor. "The *first* priority of a teaching museum," Audrey Hawthorn has written, "should be to have all objects, though kept safely, visible to students and the interested public."

All open-storage items are laid out on shelves or in drawers. Each item is numbered. Those visitors wanting more information can look it up behind corresponding numbers in bound ledgers atop the drawer stacks.

Precisely because these items are neatly laid out and the area is tidy has caused some confusion. Writes museum director Michael M. Ames: "Our visible storage

1.

1. End-on view of Museum of Anthropology's Great Hall.
2. Site drawing.

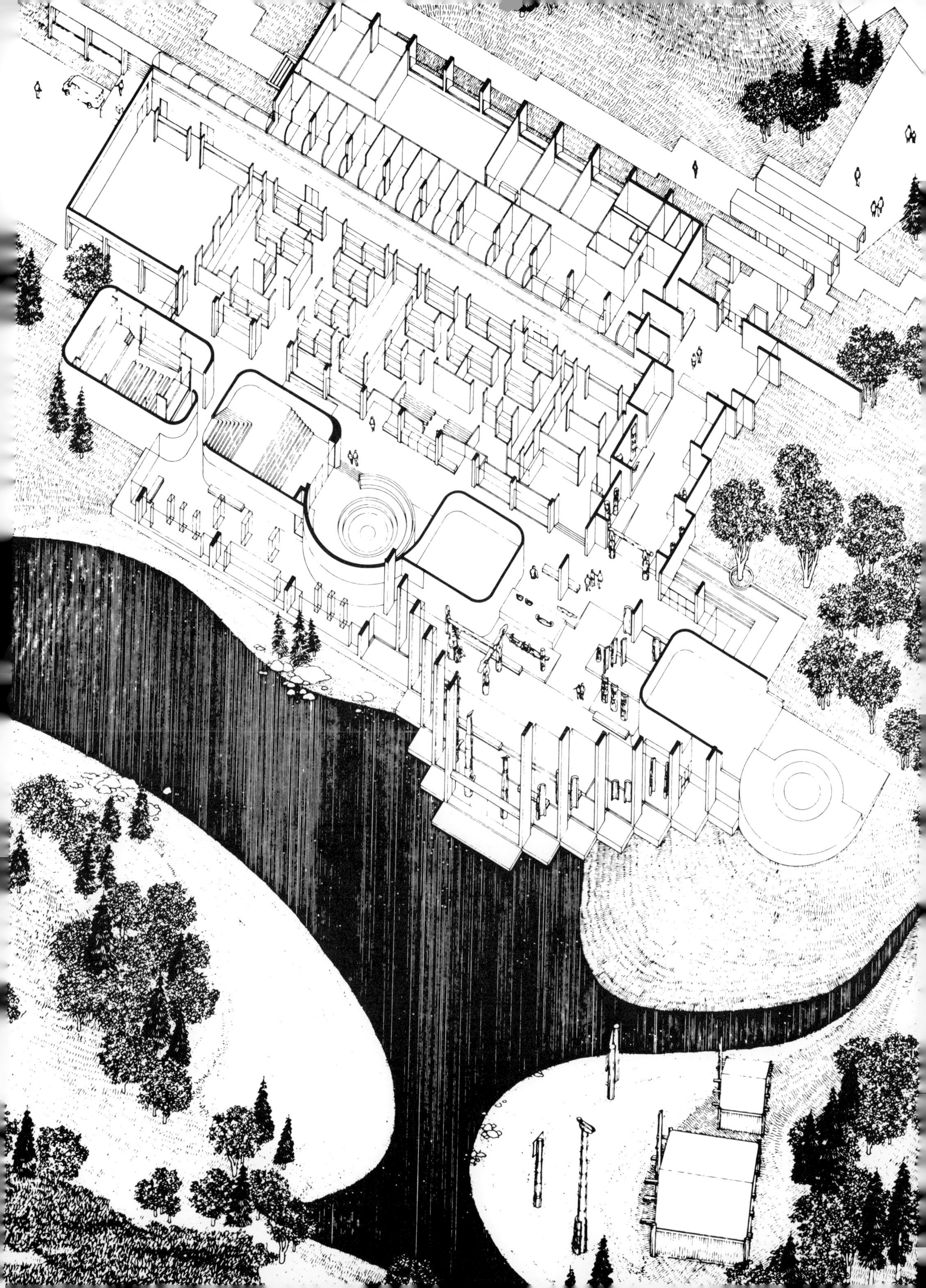

3. Giant totems in Great Hall.
4. Kwakuitl mask case.
5. Trio of totems.
6. Totems in Great Hall at sunset.
7, 8. Open storage cases.
9. Glass cases.

3.

85/Exhibition Design

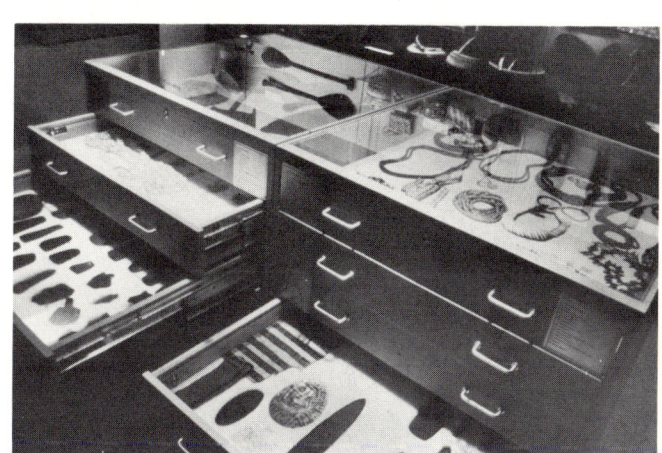

system has one serious problem: it looks too nice, too much like an exhibit to seem like storage. It is, therefore, confusing to many people who think of storage as attics, back rooms or sheds—places that are dark, dusty and inconveniently located. The visible storage area is spacious, airy and neat, and many people think they are in the midst of an exhibit area. 'Your displays are too crowded,' some have said. 'Why do you have junk next to that priceless china?' "

But the museum staff, recovering from years of having its collections packed away and inaccessible, delights in the open storage; having the storage open to all, they argue, goes a long way toward demystifying the museum.

What confusion there is can be easily overcome—by design. According to William McLennan, one of the exhibit designers, now on the museum staff, they may try defining the storage area entrance more by carefully shifting shelves or modular cases. Or they may change the sign at the entrance from "Open Storage" to "Research Collection."

Client: University of British Columbia (Vancouver, B.C.)
Design firm: Hopping, Kovach & Grinnel, Vancouver, B.C.
Designers: Rudy Kovach, Gordon Robinson, Dick Lott, Bill McLennan
Architect: Arthur Erickson Architects
Consultants: Department of Anthropology, University of British Columbia; Bogue Babicki and Associates (structural); W.T. Haggert and Co. Ltd. (electrical); Cornelia Hahn Oberlander (landscape)
Fabricators: Scali Durante Furniture Manufacturers Ltd. (displays); Grimwood Construction Co. Ltd. (general contractor); Doyle Construction Co. Ltd. (site development)

10. Indian dance performance in Great Hall.
11. Theater.

10.

11.

Exhibition Design/86

Natural Science

Philadelphia's Academy of Natural Science is distinguished, imposing, venerable. But despite its staid facade on Franklin Parkway, it is a vibrant storehouse of lore and learning whose scientists are heavily involved in current research in zoology, botany, minerology and paleontology. Academy scientists are constantly in the field studying, say, wildebeest in Africa or whales in the Sea of Cortez.

With a budget of $100,000 and a year's time, Carlos Ramirez & Albert H. Woods, Inc., set out to produce an exhibit that would clarify for visitors (school groups and general museum-goers) just what the Academy does and what natural science is. The Academy wanted the public to realize that natural science is alive and exciting and that Academy scientists do more than dust collections.

Ramirez & Woods realized right off that they needed a film to get this message across. Static displays of museum collections might go a long way toward explaining natural science, but only a film with live animals, they felt, could adequately illustrate that natural science is the study of nature and that nature is still alive and moving around.

Ramirez & Woods almost always produce their own films, and Carlos Ramirez, who enjoys the outdoors, went off with a camera to photograph wildlife in the North Woods and elsewhere in North America. What eventually emerged is a 20-minute 16mm film showing animals in their natural habitats. By dividing the material into disciplines, they explain that the study of those insects you see cavorting among flowers is called entomology; the study of fish, ichthyology; the study of snails or clams or conches, malacology, and so on.

"The film complements the rest of the exhibit," says Albert Woods. Another part of the exhibit, grouped around the motion picture screen and benches at one end of the hall, illustrates disciplines pursued by the Academy. Photos and artifacts from the collections are displayed in internally lighted cases 7' high, 4' wide and 18" deep. Welded brackets suspend these cases beneath balcony girders on two sides of the hall. Lights shining from the hanging cases' bottoms form pools on the carpet below, lighting visitors' passage among the cases and enhancing the display's floating effect. Often, two or more cases are connected, sometimes at an angle, sometimes in a straight line.

In the cases, the designers positioned transparencies of the museum's collections. "The first thing we did," explains Albert Woods, "was to photograph heavily the museum's study collections. Much of their material is too fragile or rare to go on display." Also in the internally lighted cases are photographs and actual artifacts. An occasional small artifact is placed in a translucent acrylic box and positioned among the transparencies.

Other sections deal with the Academy's history, with Academy-financed expeditions

1. Exhibit surrounds dinosaur skeleton at Academy of Natural Science.

and with great naturalists associated at one time or another with the Academy. In the latter display Ramirez and Woods positioned personal items along with photos, items once used by the scientists—eyeglasses, microscopes, etc.

In the center of all this stands the skeleton of a large dinosaur.

From time to time the exhibit lights dim and still images (of a lion, for instance) appear on the movie screen, signalling the film.

One area of the exhibit appeals particularly to children, and is meant to. It is a continuously operating slide show projected on four screens. Visitors sitting or standing in front of the screens try to identify animals by the sounds they make. If the sound alone is too difficult (and it almost always is), visual clues flash on the screen. For example, the sounds of whales calling beneath the sea is accompanied by slides of the ocean, or a close-up of a whale's eye, its hide and finally its tail flukes. Much the same is done with a grasshopper, a zebra, a frog, and a vulture.

Client: Academy of Natural Science (Philadelphia)
Design firm: Carlos Ramirez & Albert H. Woods, Inc., New York
Designers: Carlos Ramirez, Albert H. Woods
Fabricator: William Hect, Inc.

2. Multiple-screen slide show.
3, 5. Hanging display cases.
4. Floor plan.
6. Motion picture area.

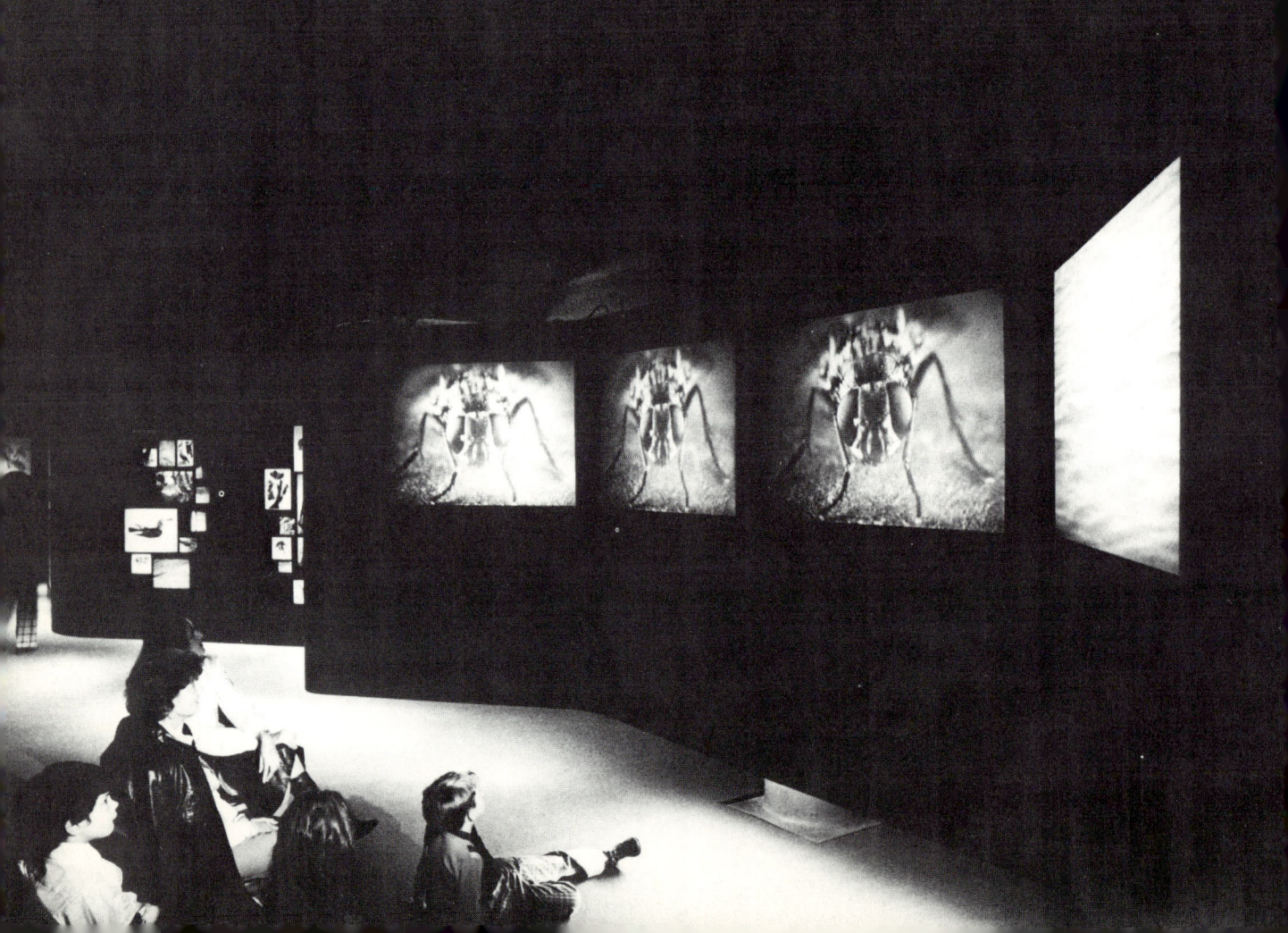

4.

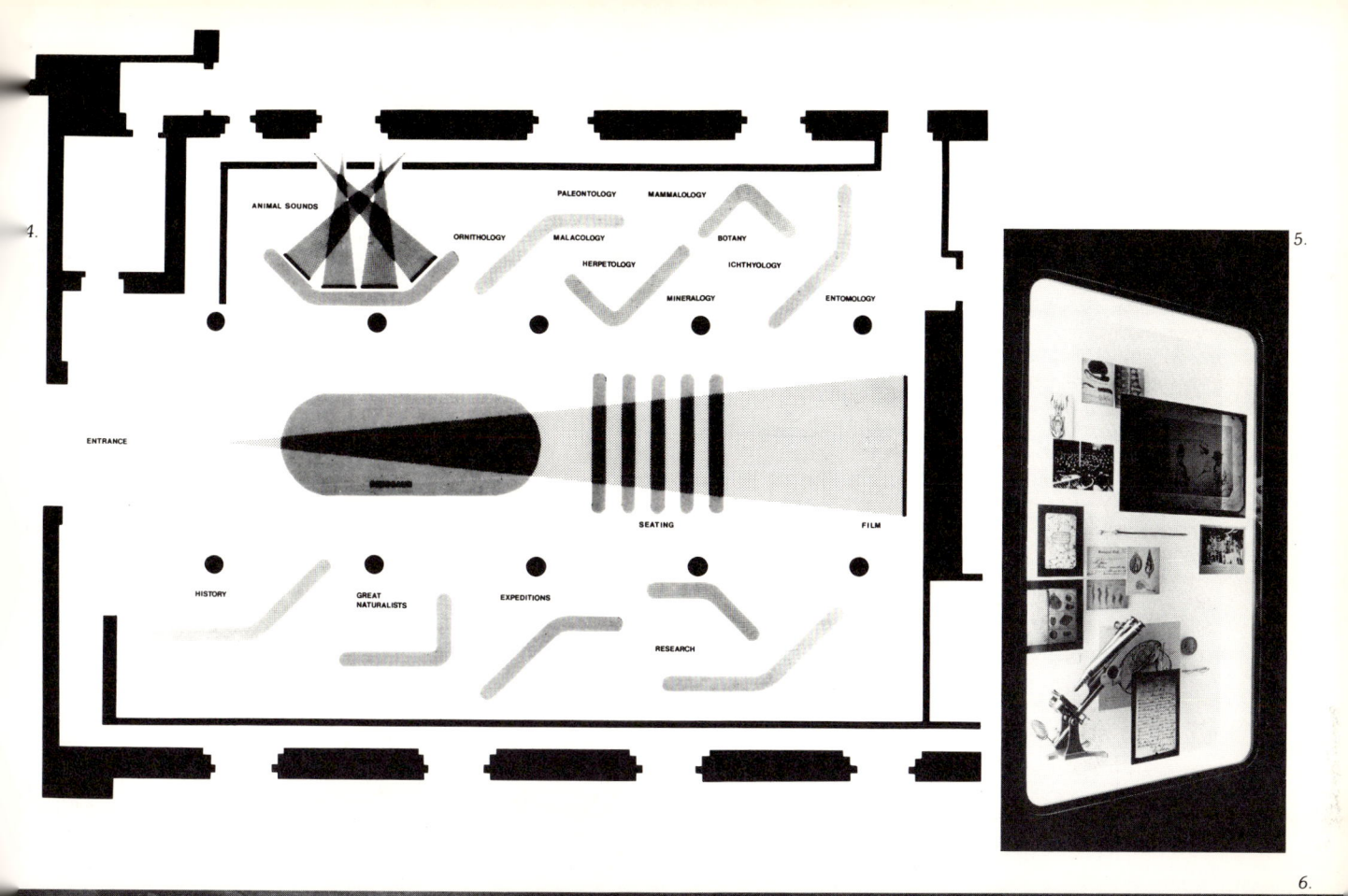

ANIMAL SOUNDS
PALEONTOLOGY MAMMALOGY
ORNITHOLOGY MALACOLOGY BOTANY
HERPETOLOGY ICHTHYOLOGY
MINERALOGY ENTOMOLOGY

ENTRANCE

SEATING FILM

HISTORY GREAT NATURALISTS EXPEDITIONS RESEARCH

5.

6.

Theatrical Set for Sports Illustrated

Mirrors have always delighted the natives. Captain Cook took mirrors to the South Pacific. Ballroom and discotheque operators suspend revolving mirrored globes above their dance floors and spot them with colored lights. Magicians use mirrors to produce illusion. Carlos Ramirez & Albert H. Woods, Inc., used them to help captivate women who buy magazine advertising space for athletic equipment manufacturers.

Sports Illustrated sponsors a theatrical trade show that tours the country playing to audiences of these women. Like most industrial trade shows, Sports Illustrated's books into hotel conference rooms and ballrooms. The act is a polished song-and-dance sales pitch; and a week before its opening, Jack Morton Productions, its producers, requested a portable setting, an environment, in which the show could go on … and on.

Using a standard, self-supporting, chromed piping system, designer Carlos Ramirez formed a scaffolding of cubic 3'6" bays. In these bays he positioned color and black-and-white photo murals of athletes in action, tilting and slanting some so that they reflected in mylar sheets, which hung from cantilevered supports 8" from the back of the chrome frame.

Ramirez placed some photos high in the 15' framework, some near the floor, some at the front, some at the back, all lighted by spots shining from the framework's top. Two of these frameworks—with lights, mylar backing and photomurals—are set up about 3½' from the walls on either side of an audience.

As the show goes on, individual photos can be spotlighted; and of course, the mylar sheets mirror the photos, chrome piping, and people in the room, extending the space and adding to the glitter.

Though Ramirez & Woods originally wanted to line the walls with mirrors, then position their framework to reflect in them, space and budget prevented it. As a final touch, the sports photos become quiz material. At the end of each show, the audience identifies individuals and events shown in some of the photos.

Like most exhibit designers, Carlos Ramirez and Albert Woods are probably showmen at heart, and Ramirez says he liked best the chance to participate in a live event, to develop a concept involved in "another medium of entertainment or communication."

Client: Jack Morton Productions (New York)
Design firm: Carlos Ramirez & Albert H. Woods, Inc., New York
Designer: Carlos Ramirez
Consultant: Tom Janus (lighting and production)
Fabricator: K & L Color (color prints); Adirondack Scenic (set construction)

1-3. Sports photos in chrome piping system, reflected in mylar sheets hanging behind the framework.

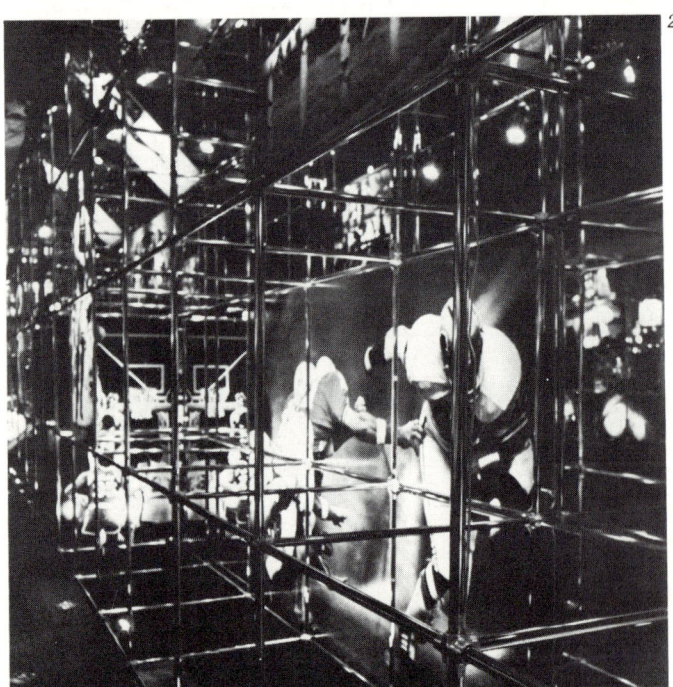

91/Exhibition Design

Egyptian Reinstallation
Phase I

By the time the Metropolitan Museum of Art completes the third and final phase of reinstalling its Egyptian collection, 45,000 objects will be on display. For the past 17 years or so the bulk of the collection has been squirreled away in research and storage areas and as much as a third of the collection has never been on public view at all. All that is changing. A recent grant from Lila Acheson Wallace, herself a collector of Egyptian art, made possible the redesign of the Metropolitan's Egyptian collection and led to the decision to display everything in the collection, long a desire of former museum director Thomas P. Hoving. By the way artifacts are grouped and lit, the exhibit's designers, the architectural firm of Kevin Roche, John Dinkeloo & Associates, will distinguish objects' relative importance. Eventually the collections will fill 23 galleries on the museum's first floor, occupying about 40,000 sq. ft., or a little over an acre.

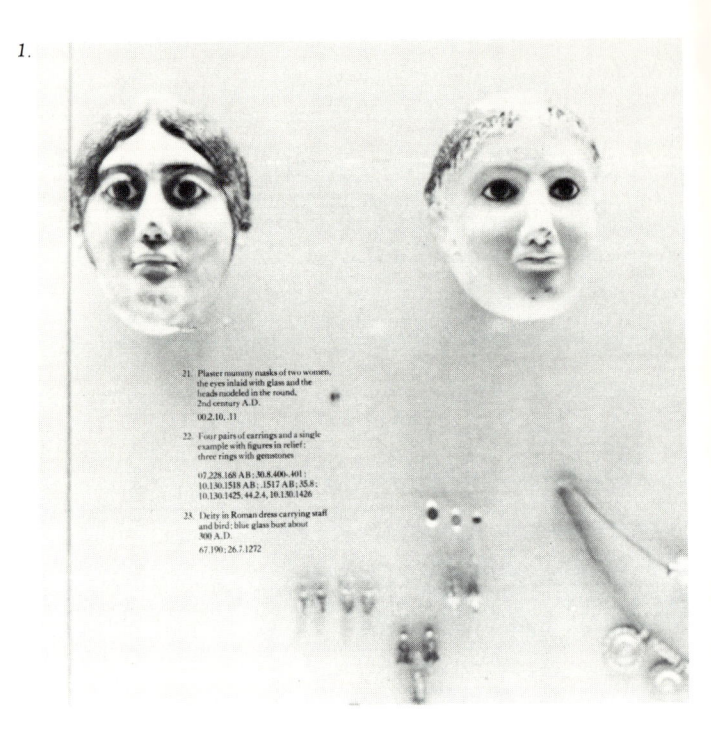

1. Plaster mummy masks and jewelry.
2. Plan.
3. Walk-in glass cases.

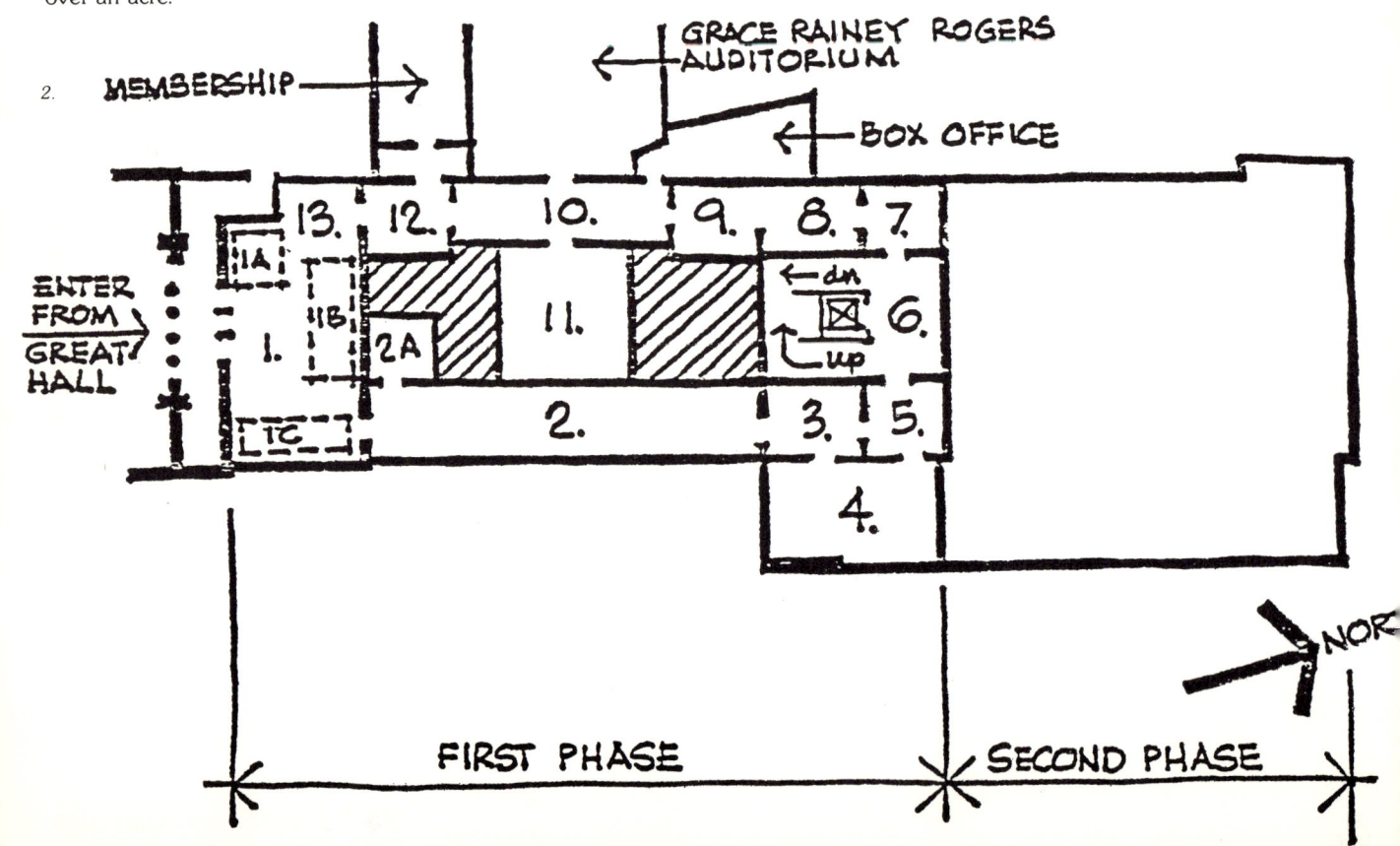

Key *(opposite)*:
1. Orientation
1a. Rauemkai
1b. Pernebi
1c. Predynastic
2. Dynasties 1-10
3. Mentuhotpe
4. Mekutra and Wah
5. Dynasty 11
6. Elevator lounge
7. Dynasty 30
8, 9. Ptolemaic
10. Grace Rainey Rogers Auditorium
11. Special Exhibition Gallery
12. Roman
13. Coptic

93/Exhibition Design

The Casebook jurors found the architects' approach to exhibit design both refreshing and sobering... refreshing in its new approaches to old problems, and sobering in that this freshness comes from outside the exhibit design profession. Roche, Dinkeloo & Associates brought the same attention to detail, the same clarity of form and the same imaginative grace to exhibits that they bring to their buildings. Not only have they handled the space with aplomb, lowering a ceiling here to provide a sense of intimacy, curving a display case there to break up the line of sight and offer surprise around a corner, but they have also paid meticulous attention to texture and color. Floors in the museum's Egyptian galleries are now a reddish granite meant to match Aswan granite. Walls are limestone as a backdrop for limestone objects; wooden carvings are placed on wooden pedestals; an overall background is linen. "We wanted to use Egyptian materials," explains Kevin Roche, "and Egyptian colors." Egypt is two colors. "When you fly over Egypt," Roche goes on, "there is the limestone color of the desert and the band of green at the edge of the Nile." This green is picked up in the carpet used, in places, throughout the exhibit. "You are left with an environment that enhances the collection's appearance," said one Casebook juror. And another noted, "The artifacts are grouped beautifully."

This grouping is partly the result of the architects' search for display devices that would give them flexibility. They didn't want to show items individually, each on its own pedestal. And "ideally," says Kevin Roche, "we would like to show objects without glass. But in the Metropolitan, with the traffic volume they have, you can't do that. So the challenge is how to show them without making them remote."

Their solution is a series of steel-framed cases, positioned against the wall, fronted by 8'-high panels of tempered glass, large enough for curators to walk into, with a 30" width left in the rear so a cart can get through carrying heavier artifacts. The largest of these cases, which have their own lighting, humidity, temperature and dust control, is 8' high, 138' long and 13½' deep. Within these cases objects can obviously be positioned with great flexibility, being clustered or spaced in two dimensions. And the cases themselves are rarely rectilinear or set flat against a wall. Rather, they flow through a series of angles and corners, creating space within the exhibit with a suppleness that keeps Roche, Dinkeloo's work from being rigid or over-romantic.

Within the exhibit each gallery has an orientation area where those who wish can study background text on what is being displayed. Rudolph de Harak designed a series of light-box tables, 4' long and 20" wide, of steel and glass (reiterating the polished steel and glass of the exhibit cases), at which vistors can sit (on bentwood chairs) or stand and read about what they are about to see. At one point de Harak mounted a 25'-long light box at eye level on a wall. Incorporating

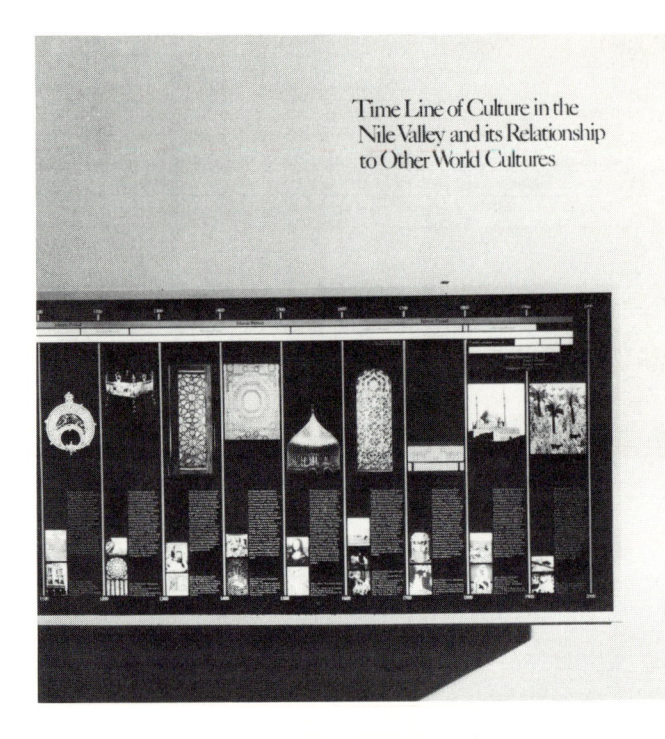

Exhibition Design/94

4. Steel and glass wall case with explanatory texts.
5. Waist-high tables with chairs encourage leisurely reading of explanatory texts.
6. Floors are reddish granite, walls are limestone.

Photos: Stan Ries (Figs. 1, 4, 5); Evelyn Hofer (all others)

95/Exhibition Design

7. Lowered ceiling above glass-encased mummy cases.
8. Some texts are silk-screened directly to glass cases.

transparencies of maps, artifacts and diagrams with large amounts of Caslon type (Caslon, he says, relates to the Metropolitan Museum of Art's image), de Harak's graphics suit both the surrounding architecture and the collection. On-site identification of artifacts is screened onto glass cases or attached to walls.

While work goes on, the unopened gallery space is used for restoration, preservation and staging. The museum decided, it should be noted, to do restoration work in a way that lets viewers know what has been restored and retouched. "In displaying ancient art, most museums use plaster to fill in voids, gaps, in original pieces of sculpture," says a museum spokesman. "The practice now, however, is to concentrate on original work and to give up the former ideal of completeness. Therefore, in this installation, old plaster in-fill has frequently been removed and replaced by new in-fill that is less strong in color and texture than the original works of art. In other objects, such as larger wall reliefs, the in-fill has been removed entirely and the fragments mounted in proper relationship, allowing the eye to supply the missing sections."

Client: The Metropolitan Museum of Art (New York); Arthur Rosenblatt, Vice Director, Architecture & Planning
Design firm: Kevin Roche, John Dinkeloo & Associates, Hamden, CT
Designers: Kevin Roche; Rudolph de Harak (graphics)
Consultants: John Altieri & Associates (mechanical engineers); Severud Associates (structural engineers)